HANDCRAFTED

Weddings

Over 100 Projects & Ideas
FOR PERSONALIZING YOUR WEDDING

CREATIVE
PUBLISHING
international

CHANHASSEN, MINNESOTA
www.creativepub.com

Copyright © 1999
Creative Publishing international, Inc.
18705 Lake Drive East
Chanhassen, Minnesota 55317
1-800-328-3895
www.creativepub.com
All rights reserved
Printed in U.S.A.

President/CEO: Michael Eleftheriou
Vice President/Publisher: Linda Ball
Vice President/Retail Sales: Kevin Haas

Created by: The Editors of Creative Publishing international, Inc.

Executive Editor: Alison Brown Cerier
Project Manager: Amy Friebe
Senior Art Director: Mark Jacobson
Assisting Art Directors: Michele Lehtis, Stephanie Michaud
Senior Editor: Linda Neubauer
Project Writer: Joan Houck
Copy Editor: Janice Cauley
Project and Prop Stylists: Christine Jahns, Coralie Sathre, Joanne Wawra
Lead Samplemaker: Arlene Dohrman
Sewing and Sample Production Staff: Margaret Andolshek, Karen Cermak, Sheila Duffy, Sharon Eklund,
  Phyllis Galbraith, Bridget Haugh, Teresa Henn, Muriel Lynch, Dolores Minkema, Nancy Sundeen
Senior Technical Photo Stylist: Bridget Haugh
Technical Photo Stylists: Jennifer Bailey, Sharon Eklund
Studio Services Manager: Marcia Chambers
Photo Services Coordinator: Carol Osterhus
Senior Photographer: Chuck Nields
Photographers: Tate Carlson, Rex Irmen, Jamey Mauk, Andrea Rugg
Photography Assistant: Greg Wallace
Set Builder: Dan Widerski
Mac Design Manager: Jon Simpson
Desktop Publishing Specialists: Patricia Goar, Brad Webster
Publishing Production Manager: Kim Gerber
Production Manager: Stasia Dorn
Production Staff: Patrick Gibson, Laura Hokkanen, Kay Wethern
Models: Madeline Bojar, Linnéa Christensen, Julie Eklund, Tim Himsel, Abigail Jacobson, Timothy Jacobson,
  Marie Kruegel, Margaret Leehe, Tracy Maloney, Betsy Neubauer, Linda Neubauer, Michelle Peterson
Consultants: Joan Bakken, Mary Holman-Allen, Jorgina Livingston, Jan Niemann, Janice Rapacz,
  Julie Rosenthal, Patricia Trumbull, Linda Wyszynski
Contributors: American Efrid, Inc., B. B. World Corporation, Desmond's Formal Wear at the Mall of America, General
  Housewares Corp., Offray Ribbon
Photography Contributors: Michael and Joannie Anderson/Anderson's Designer Portraits (pp. 167, 177); Maureen Larson,
  photographer/The Portrait Gallery (p. 167); Kevin Timian/Framework Photography (pp. 162-163)

Special thanks to the following for the use of their facilities in our location photography: Como Park Conservatory, St. Paul, MN;
  Guardian Angels Church, Chaska, MN; Our Lady of Grace, Edina, MN

Printed on American paper by:
  R. R. Donnelley
10 9 8 7 6 5 4 3 2 1

Creative Publishing international, Inc.
offers a variety of how-to books.
For information write:
        Creative Publishing international, Inc.
        Subscriber Books
        18705 Lake Drive East
        Chanhassen, MN 55317

Library of Congress Cataloging-in-Publication Data

Handcrafted Weddings : over 100 projects & ideas for personalizing
  your wedding.
        p.   cm.
    ISBN 0-86573-177-2 (hardcover); 1-58923-108-2 (softcover)
    1. Handicraft. 2. Wedding decorations. I. Creative Publishing
international.
  TT149.H36 1999
  745.594'1--dc21   99-23625

HANDCRAFTED

Weddings

Melanie and Todd

request the pleasure of your company

at the celebration of their marriage

on Saturday, the ninth of April

at two o'clock

Rosewood Country Club

210 Cliff Road

Seattle, Washington

Reception following ceremony

Please respond on or before
May 15, 200

M

number of persons

Over 100 Projects & Ideas
FOR PERSONALIZING YOUR WEDDING

TABLE OF
Contents

6   *Introduction*

9   *Wedding Stationery*
STATIONERY BASICS. 10
DECORATIVE EFFECTS 16

26   *Bridal Party Accessories*
BRIDAL VEILS 28
EDGE FINISHES 36
HEADPIECES 42
HAIR ACCESSORIES 50
BRIDAL GARTERS 63
SHOES 68
GLOVES 78
DRAWSTRING BAG 80

87 *Ceremony Accents*

FLOWER GIRL POSY BALLS 88
BASKETS 93
RING BEARER PILLOWS 96
BRIDAL & ATTENDANT BOUQUETS 102
CORSAGES & BOUTONNIERES 108
PEW ACCENTS 114
A WEDDING ARBOR 120

124 *Staging a Reception*

FRESH FLORAL TABLE WREATHS 126
MIRROR TILE CENTERPIECES 130
CARD HOLDERS 134
CHAMPAGNE BOTTLE COVER 138
CAKE TOPS 142
SLIPCOVERED CHAIRS 146
TABLE FAVORS 148
TABLE SKIRTS 156

161 *Cherished Memorabilia*

FABRIC-COVERED PICTURE FRAMES 162
FABRIC-COVERED PHOTO ALBUMS,
GUEST BOOKS & VIDEO CASES 168
DRIED WEDDING WREATH 178
HEIRLOOM SHADOW BOX 184

190 *Index*

SOURCES 192

HANDCRAFTED WEDDINGS
Introduction

Weddings are very personal, with every detail carefully pondered and carried out to perfection. You'd love to be extravagant with every aspect, but good sense tells you to save a little money for life after the wedding. With a little creativity, you can have the wedding of your dreams at an affordable price. Handcrafted items, like veils and headpieces, flower girl baskets and bridal bouquets, are unique, and they can be made at a fraction of the cost of purchased items.

The projects in this book take you through designing and creating your own wedding stationery, accessorizing the wedding party, decorating the ceremony and reception sites, and preserving your cherished memories. And because individuality is key, we offer lots of variations so you can select a style that fits your idea of the perfect wedding.

While coordinating the necessary arrangements for your wedding, when would you find time to make all of these beautiful things, too? Delegate! Many friends and family members would be honored if you asked them to help. Plan a weekend get-together with your groom and both sets of parents to help you prepare and send invitations. Assemble your bridesmaids for an evening of girl talk and crafting reception centerpieces. Perhaps ask a favorite aunt to make a ring bearer pillow or sew your garter. Remember that many items can be crafted long in advance of the wedding, preserving your sanity in the last few weeks or giving you time for last-minute flower preparation.

Select the projects that mean the most to you. Weigh the money savings, uniqueness, and personal satisfaction in making a project against the time commitment required. Even if the only item you make is your own headpiece and veil, you could save enough money to purchase gifts for your bridesmaids. Each item you create marks another joyful moment leading to your special day.

WEDDING STATIONERY

Handcrafted wedding invitations and thank-you cards set the tone for your unique wedding. Designed by the bride and groom, they offer guests a personal touch that can't be equaled.

STATIONERY
Basics

From invitations to thank-you cards, handmade wedding stationery conveys your sentiments with personal flair.

There are many paper options and methods for embellishment to choose from. Start with purchased cards, or create your own from card or paper stock, available from stationery, art, or craft stores. Print your message, and embellish the cards as lavishly or as simply as you wish. Consider a variety of effects, including pressure embossing, stamping, thermal embossing, stenciling, and watercolor painting. Create interest with deckled or die-cut edges. Incorporate other elements, such as ribbons, pressed flowers, or feathers.

Stock used for printing can become the base card, or the printed copies can be cut and mounted to other paper. The paper stock on which the message is to be printed must have a smooth texture and be of medium weight, such as laser-printable papers, card stock, or vellum, and it must be of a standard printing size. Compose and lay out the message on a computer; then either print copies onto the chosen stock, using a laser printer, or print out a copy on white paper and have a professional printer reproduce it.

*Please respond on or before
May 15, 2001*

M

number of persons

Reception and dan
immediately following

Glendale
612 Valley View
Bloomingto

SELECTING PAPERS

Wedding stationery can be created from ready-made cards or cut from paper or card stock. For ready-made cards, select plain blank cards with matching envelopes or those imprinted with a simple design that could be further embellished. Add details, such as a stenciled border design, an edging, or an embossed design.

Cut your own cards from a wide variety of papers; browse through art supply, stationery, and craft stores, or visit a professional printer for papers. Parchment, card and cover stock, and watercolor paper are a few options. Handmade papers, which have a lovely nubby surface, may have flower petals, leaves, or metallic strings embedded in them. Since many textured papers do not take to printing, print messages on other stock and mount them to the textured paper.

Whether you choose ready-made cards or cut them from stock, you can create interesting effects by layering papers of various textures. Translucent overlays, such as tissue, vellum, and Japanese lace paper, are lovely options as well.

1 Decide on the desired components of the wedding stationery. Besides the invitation and mailing envelope, consider an inner envelope to hold the invitation and all the inserts, a response card with an envelope, a reception card, and a thank-you card with an envelope.

2 Plan the size and format of the cards. Not all the pieces of the set need to be exactly the same, but they should have a common design element. Invitations and insert cards can be a single, heavy card or a double-folded sheet. If cards will be cut to size, consider sizes of available envelopes. Cards should be ¼" (6 mm) shorter and narrower than the accompanying envelope.

3 Print message on standard-size paper; trim to desired size.

4 Cut several sheets of paper at once, using paper cutter or rotary cutter, straightedge, and cutting mat. Cut decorative edges, if desired, using specialty rotary cutter blades or scissors with decorative-edged blades. Or, tear deckled edges (page 22).

5 Mark lightly for any folds. For heavy paper, lightly score foldline on outside, using back of mat knife blade. For mediumweight and lightweight papers, burnish foldline on inside, using butter knife or stylus.

ATTACHING OVERLAYS

RIBBON & SEALING WAX

Fold two papers in half, place one inside the other, and wrap decorative string or ribbon around fold. Secure overlay to main card stock with sealing wax. Light wick of wax stick, hold stick at an angle, and drip wax over area to be sealed. Push stamp into wax, imprinting design, if desired. Wax seals may break if mailed.

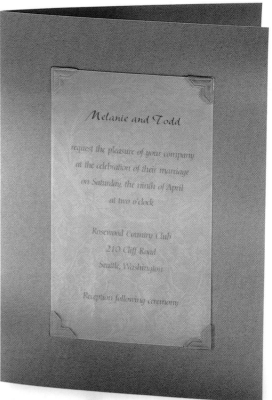

MOUNTING CORNERS

Secure corners of overlay, using self-adhesive paper mounting corners.

GLUE STICK

Fold a full-card overlay in half. Apply glue to wrong side of overlay back; slip main card stock inside, and press to secure. Leave front overlay loose, or attach to front corners with glue stick.

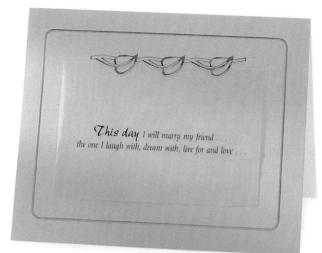

STICKERS

Secure edges of single overlay with three-dimensional self-adhesive paper stickers.

CRAFT GLUE

Apply a drop of glue between overlay and main card stock at top edge of overlay. Ease excess glue above overlay; secure bow or charm.

AEROSOL ADHESIVE

Attach sheer paper to solid-color backing paper, using aerosol adhesive. Trim to size after layering.

WOVEN RIBBON

Punch two holes through both layers of paper. Run ribbon ends through holes from underside, as shown. Tie the ribbon in a simple knot or bow, if desired. Trim tails at an angle.

DECORATIVE *Effects*

*Design unique wedding stationery with a
personal touch, using easy decorative techniques.*

Add elegant textural interest to cards with embossed designs. Select either subtle pressure embossing, using a brass embossing plate and a stylus, or thermal embossing, using a rubber stamp and special embossing powders.

Embellish with colorful stenciled designs, using an ink pad and makeup sponges. Or develop one-of-a-kind watercolor effects with paint and kosher salt.

Create unusual shapes, cutouts, or edges with die-cutting techniques. For fine finishing detail, deckle the edges, using a specially designed ruler. Or, weave an elegant narrow ribbon through tiny slits in the paper.

Your personal style may include more than one of these techniques. All the supplies you need are available at art supply or stationery stores, or through mail-order sources.

Melanie and Todd
request the pleasure of your company
at the celebration of their marriage
on Saturday, the ninth of April
at two o'clock
Rosewood Country Club
210 Cliff Road
Seattle, Washington
Reception following ceremony

Pressure Embossing

YOU WILL NEED

- CARD STOCK OR HEAVYWEIGHT PAPER
- EMBOSSING PLATE
- BALL-TIP STYLUS
- REMOVABLE TAPE
- LIGHT BOX OR OTHER ILLUMINATED GLASS SURFACE

1 Cut paper to desired size, or use purchased card. Print message on paper or card, if message is desired on the embossed paper.

2 Tape embossing plate to light box. Or, place small lamp under glass-top table; tape embossing plate to tracing paper, and tape to glass.

3 Place card or paper, wrong side up, over plate in desired position. Tape card edges down, using removable tape. Test tape on scrap paper first, to be sure it won't damage paper.

4 Trace outline of design with stylus; apply firm pressure. If stylus squeaks during use, lubricate the end by rubbing it in the palm of your hand. Remove tape.

Stamping Designs

YOU WILL NEED
- INK PAD
- STAMP

1 Cut paper to desired size, or use purchased card. Print message on paper or card, if message is desired on the stamped paper.

2 Press stamp firmly onto stamp pad; lift and repeat as necessary until design on stamp is evenly coated with ink. Press stamp straight down onto card front or paper, using even pressure.

Thermal Embossing

YOU WILL NEED
- RUBBER STAMP
- EMBOSSING INK PAD
- EMBOSSING POWDER
- HEAT SOURCE, SUCH AS A LIGHT BULB OR HEAT GUN

1 Follow steps 1 and 2, above, using embossing ink. Sprinkle with embossing powder while ink is still wet; shake off all excess powder.

2 Hold paper near heat source, such as a light bulb or heat gun, until all powder melts, forming raised design.

Stenciling

You will need
- Ink pads in desired colors
- Makeup sponges
- Stencil
- Removable tape

1 Cut paper to desired size, or use purchased card. Print message on paper or card, if message is desired on the painted paper.

2 Secure stencil over paper, using removable tape. Press makeup sponge onto ink pad.

3 Apply ink to paper, using a pouncing motion; replenish ink as needed. Use new sponge for each additional color, overlapping and blending colors as desired.

Painting with Watercolors

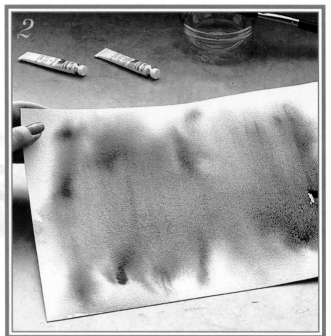

YOU WILL NEED

- WATERCOLOR PAPER OR PURCHASED CARDS OF WATERCOLOR PAPER
- 1 TO 3 TUBES OF LIGHT SHADES OF WATERCOLOR PAINT
- PAINTBRUSHES
- KOSHER SALT
- PALETTE OR SMALL DISHES

Dampen paper with water. Squeeze paint onto palette. Mix desired color, if necessary. Wet brush and dilute paint with water.

1

Apply diluted paint to paper in broad random strokes. If more than one color is desired, use different brush for each color. Tilt and turn paper to distribute paint to desired areas.

2

Lay paper flat. Sprinkle kosher salt sparingly over wet paint. Allow to dry.

3

Brush salt from completely dry paper. Cut paper to desired size.

4

3

YOU WILL NEED

- MAT KNIFE; CUTTING MAT
- TEMPLATE OR STENCIL, OPTIONAL
- STRAIGHTEDGE, OPTIONAL

Cut paper to desired size, or use purchased card.

1

2 Choose design for diecut. The larger or simpler the design, the easier it is to cut out. When cutting out a rectangle or square, straight inside corners are easier to cut than rounded ones.

3 Embellish card as desired. Trace area to be cut, using stencil or template, unless area will be cut freehand.

4 Cut out design, using a mat knife; use template or straightedge to cut straight lines.

4

Wedding Stationery

Making a Deckled Edge

YOU WILL NEED
- ART DECKLE® RULER

 Print message on paper, if message is desired on the deckle-edged paper. Place paper right side down on work surface.

 Dampen ¾" (2 cm) edge of watercolor or heavier-weight paper, using clean paintbrush and water. For lightweight paper, such as bond, omit this step.

 Place Art Deckle ruler ½" (1.3 cm) from edge of paper; hold firmly in place. Slowly tear ½" (1.3 cm) edge off, pulling it against edge of ruler.

 Remove ruler. Smooth edge outward; allow to dry.

Weaving Ribbon

YOU WILL NEED

- Ribbon
- Chenille or tapestry needle, for weaving narrow ribbon
- Paper clip, for weaving wider ribbon
- Mat knife
- Cutting mat

1 Cut paper to desired size, or use purchased card. Print message on paper or card, if message is desired on paper with woven ribbon. Embellish as desired.

2 Mark two horizontal lines on paper where ribbon is desired, using a light pencil mark. Distance between lines is slightly more than width of ribbon.

3 Between marked lines, cut vertical pairs of slits, using mat knife and cutting mat. For a narrow ribbon, cut slits in each pair about ⅛" (3 mm) apart, and space pairs 1" (2.5 cm) apart; for wider ribbon, increase distances.

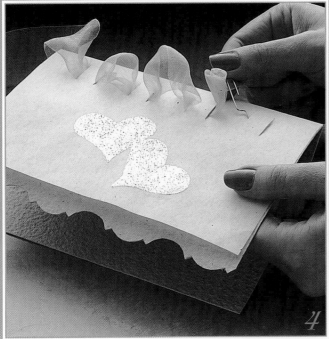

4 Weave ribbon under each pair of slits and over spaces between pairs. Thread narrow ribbon into a chenille or tapestry needle for weaving; for wider ribbon, poke ribbon through slits using the end of an unfolded paper clip.

Tip

When buying postage, choose a stamp that complements your stationery. For additional options, ask to see the commemorative stamps.

Variations

ON THE THEME

PRESSED FLOWER

Create a diecut opening to overlay and frame a pressed pansy, delicately displayed on handmade paper and covered with fine tulle. Tie sheer ribbon into a bow and glue to the card front.

SHEER WRAP

Wrap simple invitations with sheer decorative tissue paper, for a classy, but very easy, touch. Tie the wrap in place with sheer ribbon.

This day I will marry my friend . . .
. . . laugh with, dream with, live for and love . . .

FEATHER ACCENT

Attach a vellum overlay to watercolored paper by running a slender feather through diagonal slits cut in the papers.

Julia Engel and Michael Beck

request the pleasure

of your company

as they join in marriage

Saturday, the third of June

at two o'clock

2124 Fern Drive

Bloomington, Minnesota

SEPIA TONES

Print your message in sepia ink on a vellum overlay. Attach the overlay to preprinted sepia-toned paper, using a dot of glue on a gilded silk leaf.

BRIDAL PARTY ACCESSORIES

Designed to complement the gowns, perfect accessories are both affordable and easy to make. Creative details express your style, from stunning headpieces to customized shoes.

BRIDAL
Veils

Bridal veils are easy to make, and the cost savings are substantial.

Try on several veils to determine the style and length that are most flattering to you. Many stores that carry veil and headpiece supplies have samples available. In general, the more elaborate the gown, the simpler the veil and headpiece.

Use the chart on page 30 to determine the desired length of the veil. Consider the formality of the wedding and the style of the back of the dress. If the veil is shorter than floor length, plan for it to end below the design features on the back of the dress, such as a low V neck, peplum, or bow; the dress details will be visible through the sheer net. Be sure to select a veil style that works well with the headpiece (pages 42 to 49) to which it will be attached.

Nylon illusion is the most popular choice for bridal veils; it is generally available in 78" and 108" (198 and 274.5 cm) widths, and in several shades of white and ivory. Use the narrower width for shorter veils with less fullness; use the wider width for floor-length and blusher veils. Create a designer look by accenting the veil edges, using one of the methods on pages 36 to 41.

The bouffant cascade veil (left) is cut 12" (30.5 cm) higher at the center top of the veil to allow it to rise above the head, supported by an underpouf. Dropping to ballet length, the veil is edged with pearl cotton. Narrow satin binding encases the edges of the elbow-length blusher veil (opposite, left). After the ceremony, the blusher is turned back over the headpiece, forming two tiers. The fullness of the two-tier cascade veil (opposite, center) is emphasized by its rippled edge finish; the tiers are cut to shoulder and elbow lengths. The fingertip cascade veil (opposite, right) is topped with a pouf, drawing more attention to the headpiece, while delicate 1/16" (1.5 mm) ribbon defines the veil edge.

Making an Underpouf Support

1 Cut tulle 8" to 12" (20.5 to 30.5 cm) wide and 1½ yd. (1.4 m) long. Fold in half lengthwise. Hand-stitch gathering row ¼" (6 mm) from long cut edges, using double strand of thread.

2 Pull up gathers until length is 5" (12.5 cm). Stitch to top underside of veil at center. Separate layers of underpouf to billow up under veil.

*B*RIDAL VEIL LENGTHS

DESCRIPTION	LENGTH
SHOULDER OR FLYAWAY	TOUCHES SHOULDERS; WORN WITH INFORMAL GOWNS
ELBOW	TOUCHES ELBOWS WHEN ARMS ARE STRAIGHT AT THE SIDES
FINGERTIP	TOUCHES FINGERTIPS WHEN ARMS ARE STRAIGHT AT THE SIDES
BALLET OR WALTZ	FALLS TO THE ANKLES
CHAPEL	FALLS ABOUT 2½ YD. (2.3 M) FROM HEADPIECE
CATHEDRAL	FALLS ABOUT 3½ YD. (3.2 M) FROM THE HEADPIECE; USUALLY WORN WITH A CATHEDRAL TRAIN

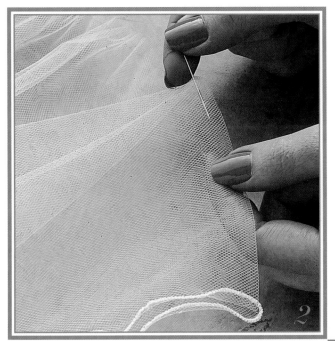

Cut net with length equal to combined length of each tier plus 6" (15 cm) for each tier, if underpouf support will be used. Fold net in half lengthwise; for two-tier veil, fold in half again, crosswise. Cut rounded corners. Apply edge finish (page 36), if desired.

1

Hand-stitch a gathering row about ¼" (6 mm) from upper edge of net, using double thread. For two tiers, fold net and stitch gathering row ¼" (6 mm) from fold.

2

3 Make headpiece (page 42). Pull up gathering row to fit headpiece. If desired, make underpouf support, opposite, and attach to underside of veil.

4 Attach veil to headpiece with hand stitches. Or, for a removable veil, cut strip of hook and loop tape to length of gathered edge. Stitch hook strip to top of veil, either to right or wrong side, depending on how it attaches to headpiece; attach loop strip to headpiece, using fabric glue.

1   Determine desired height of pouf by test-folding a length of net; hand-gather 4" to 8" (10 to 20.5 cm) from folded edge. Position gathered net at back of headpiece; adjust height of pouf, and record.

2   Cut net with length equal to combined length of each tier plus twice the height of pouf. Fold net and cut rounded corners as on page 31, step 1.

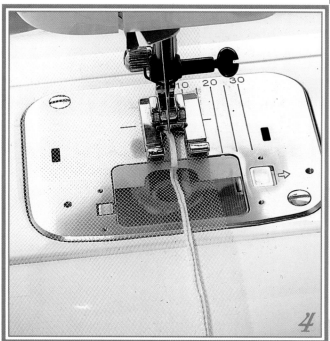

Fold net at desired height of pouf and length of upper tier; on both sides of veil, place pins at bottom of pouf on lower tier, near edges. Omit step 4 if edge finish is not desired.   *3*

Apply edge finish, page 36, to right side of lower tier, between pin marks. Apply finish to reverse side of pouf and upper tier; when upper tier is folded over, trim will be on top side of veil. Or, omit edge finish in pouf.   *4*

5 Refold veil as in step 3. Using double strand of thread, hand-stitch a gathering row through both layers, with distance from folded edge equal to height of pouf.

6 Make headpiece (page 42) and attach veil as on page 31, step 4. Adjust pouf by separating layers of net.

Tip

BRING A STORAGE BOX OR BAG, IF YOU PLAN TO DETACH THE VEIL·FOR THE RECEPTION. TO REMOVE ONLY THE VEIL, LEAVING THE POUF ATTACHED TO THE HEADPIECE, CONSTRUCT THEM AS TWO SEPARATE PIECES. ATTACH THE POUF FIRST WITH HAND STITCHES; ATTACH THE VEIL WITH HOOK AND LOOP TAPE.

Making a Bouffant Veil

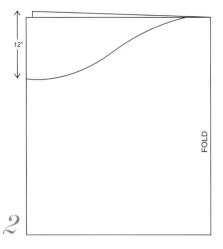

1 Measure finished length of each tier from point of attachment; add 12" (30.5 cm) for bouffant effect. Cut net for each tier; align upper edges.

2 Fold net in half lengthwise. Place pin 12" (30.5 cm) from top on cut edge. Mark gently curved line from pin to top, ending at fold. Cut along curved line.

3 Align bottom edges of tiers, and cut rounded corners as on page 31, step 1. Apply edge finish (page 36), if desired.

4 Hand-stitch gathering row ¼" (6 mm) from upper edge of net, using double thread.

5 Make headpiece (page 42). Pull up gathering row to fit headpiece. If desired, attach underpouf support (page 30). Attach veil to headpiece as on page 31, step 4.

Determine combined length of front blusher and back tier, measuring from where veil will be attached to headpiece; blusher should fall at bustline. Cut net to this length, adding 6" (15 cm) if an underpouf support will be used.

1

Fold net in half lengthwise, then in half crosswise. Cut rounded corners. Apply edge finish (page 36), if desired.

2

3 Hand-stitch a 72" (183 cm) gathering row in center portion of veil, with distance from front edge equal to length of blusher; this leaves equal ungathered areas at sides of veil.

4 Make headpiece (page 42). Pull up gathers to fit headpiece. Attach veil as on page 31, step 4.

Tip

EXPERIMENT WITH HOW YOU WILL STYLE YOUR HAIR WHEN WEARING YOUR VEIL. FOR SUGGESTIONS, TAKE YOUR VEIL TO A SALON. WHETHER YOU STYLE YOUR HAIR YOURSELF OR HAVE IT DONE PROFESSIONALLY, TESTING VARIOUS LOOKS BEFOREHAND MEANS ONE LESS DECISION ON YOUR WEDDING DAY.

EDGE *Finishes*

Edge finishes give the veil a designer look.
Delicate, soft, or tailored, they help establish
the style of the veil.

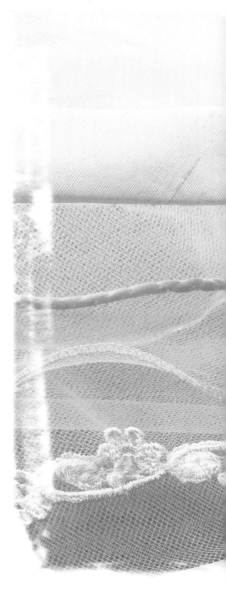

Encase edges in bias binding for a bold, tailored finish. Choose a very lightweight natural-fiber fabric, like silk shantung, which will hold a pressed edge and easily conform to curves. Make binding with a finished width of ¼" to 1½" (6 mm to 3.8 cm); the wider the edging, the bolder the look.

To estimate the number of yards (meters) of bias strip needed, add the lengths of the sides and bottom edges of each tier and divide by 36" (91.5 cm). Consult the chart below for an estimate of the length of bias strip a square of fabric will yield.

Daintily outline the lower edge with satin rattail, #5 pearl cotton, or narrow ribbon. Or, apply narrow lace edging to complement your gown. For a soft, curving look, consider a rippled edge, achieved by zigzagging or serging over fishline while stretching the veil. Select 20-pound-test fishline for firm ripples.

*B*IAS STRIP YIELDS FROM 44" (112 CM) SQUARE

FINISHED WIDTH	CUT WIDTH	YIELD
¼" (6 MM)	1" (2.5 CM)	54 YD. (49.7 M)
½" (1.3 CM)	2" (5 CM)	27 YD. (24.8 M)
¾" (2 CM)	3" (7.5 CM)	18 YD. (16.5 M)
1" (2.5 CM)	4" (10 CM)	13 YD. (11.9 M)
1¼" (3.2 CM)	5" (12.5 CM)	10¾ YD. (9.9 M)
1½" (3.8 CM)	6" (15 CM)	9 YD. (8.25 M)

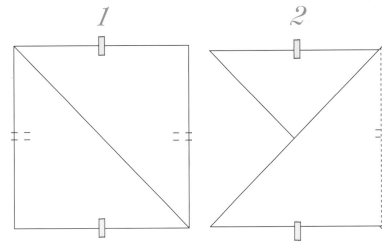

Making a Continuous Bias Binding Strip

1 Cut a 44" (112 cm) square of fabric; trim off selvages. Mark upper and lower edges of square with tape; mark left and right edges with pins. Cut diagonally from top left corner to bottom right corner.

2 Flip left triangle over vertically onto right triangle, right sides together, aligning pin-marked edges; pin, and stitch together, using ¼" (6 mm) seam allowance. Press seam open.

Continued

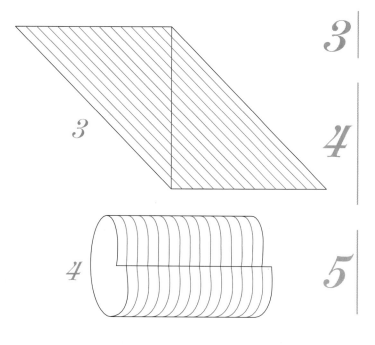

3 Mark lines across fabric parallel to long diagonal edges, with width as determined in chart (page 36).

4 Align straight-grain edges, right sides together, offsetting marks by one strip width. Stitch, and press seam open. Cut around tube on marked lines, cutting one continuous bias strip. Wrap bias strip loosely onto cardboard for easy use.

5 To attach two continuous bias strips, place ends of strips, right sides together, at a right angle; stitch on the lengthwise grain, as shown. Trim seam to ¼" (6 mm); press seam open.

Applying Bias Binding Using Sewing and Gluing Method

1 Feed bias strip into bias tape maker, using a pin to get it started. Strip will fold into binding as it is pulled through bias tape maker; press folds into place. With iron resting on binding, gently slide bias tape maker down length of strip; press, but do not stretch bias binding.

2 Press binding in half lengthwise, encasing folds. Wrap binding onto cardboard for easier handling.

3 Press-shape binding to fit veil edge without puckering. Align raw edge of binding to edge of veil, right sides together. Stitch in well of fold.

Fold binding over edge of veil to wrong side, aligning top and bottom folds of binding. Dilute flexible fabric glue to spreading consistency. Working in small sections, slip paper towel under raw edge of binding; lightly brush glue onto binding. Reposition, and finger-press in place.

4

Applying Bias Binding Using Sewing Method

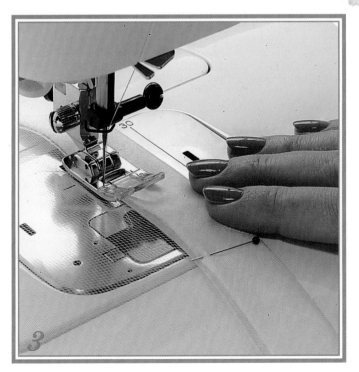

Follow step 1, opposite. Press binding in half lengthwise, encasing folds, offsetting one edge by ⅛" (3 mm). Wrap binding onto cardboard for easier handling.

1

Press-shape binding to fit veil edge without puckering, with shorter fold on right side. Align raw edge of short side of binding to raw edge of veil, right sides together. Stitch in well of fold.

2

Fold wider side of binding over edge of veil to wrong side. Stitch in the ditch from right side, catching the binding on the back of veil.

3

Sewing a Rippled Edge by Conventional Machine

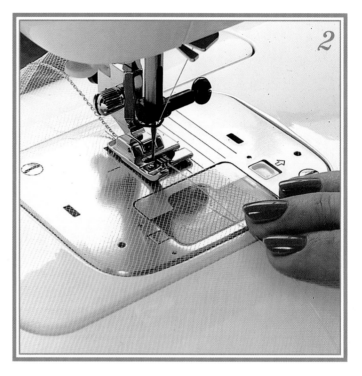

1   Set machine for narrow zigzag stitch. Attach cording foot, if available. At top of veil, place fishline ½ " (1.3 cm) from veil edge, leaving a long tail.

2   Stitch over fishline, stretching veil as you stitch; overlap ends. Trim veil close to stitching; do not cut fishline from reel.

3   Spread veil over fishline, rippling veil as desired; work from center toward ends. Seal ends with liquid fray preventer; trim fishline.

Sewing a Rippled Edge by Serger

1   Adjust serger for rolled hem stitch; attach gimp foot, if available. Insert fishline through gimp foot (or under back and over front of regular presser foot); leave long tail. Stitch over fishline about 4" (10 cm).

2   Place veil under presser foot, ½ " (1.3 cm) from edge; stitch, trimming excess veil and keeping fishline between needle and knives, if using regular presser foot.

3   Stitch over fishline 4" (10 cm) at end; do not cut fishline from reel. Follow step 3, above.

Sewing a Satin Rattail or Pearl Cotton Edge

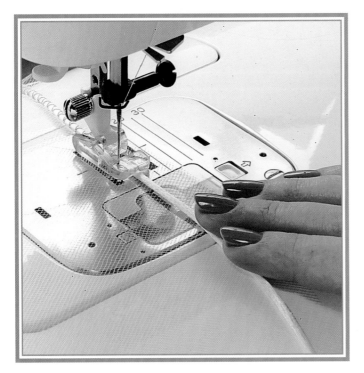

Thread machine with monofilament nylon thread in the top and bobbin. Set machine for zigzag stitch, just wide enough to pass over desired trim. Position rattail or pearl cotton ½" (1.3 cm) from edge of veil. Stitch over rattail or pearl cotton; overlap ends, and seal them with glue. Trim veil close to stitching.

Sewing a Ribbon or Lace Edge

Place ribbon or lace ½" (1.3 cm) from edge of veil. Stitch, using straight or zigzag stitch; overlap ends. Trim veil close to stitching.

Tip

PACK AN EMERGENCY KIT TO TAKE WITH YOU TO THE ROOM WHERE YOU WILL DRESS FOR THE WEDDING. INCLUDE ITEMS SUCH AS SAFETY PINS, NEEDLE AND THREAD, BOBBY PINS, DOUBLE-SIDED TAPE, MAKEUP, HAIR SPRAY, AND EXTRA HOSIERY.

Bridal Party Accessories

Headpieces

The perfect headpiece coordinates beautifully with the gown, reflects the bride's personality, and flatters her in every way.

Headpieces are available in a variety of styles and may be a wire frame or a buckram form. Choose a style that is flattering to your face shape, height, head size, and hair style, and one that will work well with the style veil you have in mind.

Select fabric for covering the headpiece that matches the wedding gown as closely as possible. Also, select the same style of embellishments, like laces, pearls, sequins, or ribbon roses.

Use a thick, white craft glue or fabric glue for making headpieces and hats; a glue that sets up quickly is easiest to work with. Most embellishments, such as lace, appliqués,

and pearls, can be secured with glue. Pearl or flower sprays and net embellishments are best hand-stitched in place.

Adjust the size of a wire frame before embellishing it, if necessary. Simply untwist or cut the wires at the back, overlap, and retwist them. To provide a base for the embellishments, wire-frame headpieces are first covered with horsehair braid, available 3" and 6" (7.5 and 15 cm) wide. Elasticized button looping is used for securing plastic combs and bobby pins to a headpiece or hat; purchase a heavyweight button looping for maximum strength.

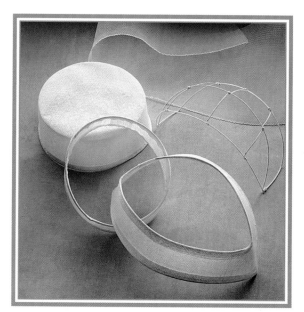

HEADPIECES & HATS
These include buckram forms, buckram pillbox hats, buckram bun wraps, and wire frames. Wide horsehair braid with a gathering cord on one side is used for covering wire frames.

Covering a Buckram Headpiece

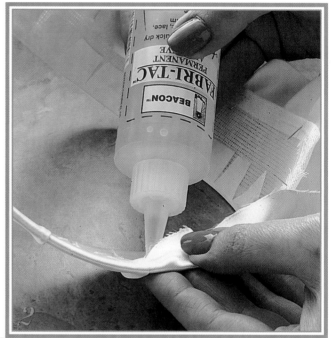

1 Cut a bias piece of fabric 1" to 2" (2.5 to 5 cm) larger than headpiece. Centering fabric on top of headpiece, smooth fabric down toward edges of headpiece; secure with pins.

2 Wrap fabric to inside of headpiece, and secure with glue, trimming and clipping fabric, and making small tucks for a smooth fit. Allow to dry, and remove pins. Glue lace trim over inside raw edge.

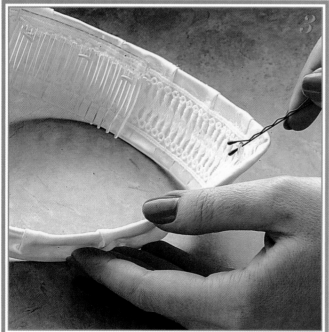

3 Cut a length of button looping slightly longer than hair comb; glue to inside of frame near front, with loops facing back of frame. Slide teeth of comb into loops. Glue one loop of button looping to each side of headpiece, and insert bobby pins. If detachable veil is desired, glue loop side of hook and loop tape to underside of headpiece where veil will be attached.

4 Cut lace motifs; apply liquid fray preventer to any cut cords on lace. Arrange lace and any additional embellishments on the headpiece as desired; secure with glue or hand stitching.

5 Apply beads and sequins, if desired; using tweezers, dip bead in glue, and secure.

1 Cut fabric circle 1" to 2" (2.5 to 5 cm) larger than top of hat. Center fabric on top of hat, and smooth fabric over sides; secure with pins. Glue fabric at sides, near top of hat, removing pins; allow to dry. Trim away excess fabric.

2 Press pleats in bias strip of fabric, folding pleats so upper raw edge is concealed. Length of pleated strip should be distance around hat plus 1" (2.5 cm) for overlap; width should be height of crown plus 1" (2.5 cm) for wrapping fabric to inside of hat.

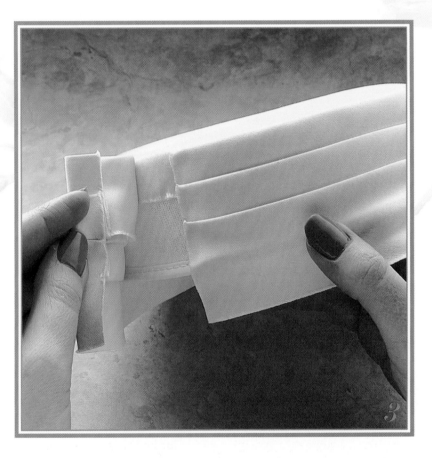

3 Glue pleated strip to crown, aligning top folded edge to top edge of hat; fold under one end and lap over other end to conceal raw edge of fabric.

4 Wrap lower edge of pleated strip to inside of hat; secure with glue. Glue lace trim over raw edge. Complete headpiece as in step 3, opposite; embellish as desired.

1 Cut bias strip of fabric 1" (2.5 cm) wider than bun wrap form with length equal to distance around form plus 1" (2.5 cm) for overlap. Wrap fabric around form, so it extends ½" (1.3 cm) beyond each edge; pin in place. Fold under one short end of fabric, and lap it over other end, concealing raw edge. Pin overlapped ends.

2 Fold fabric edges to inside of form; glue in place. Allow to dry, and remove pins. Glue lace over raw edges of fabric.

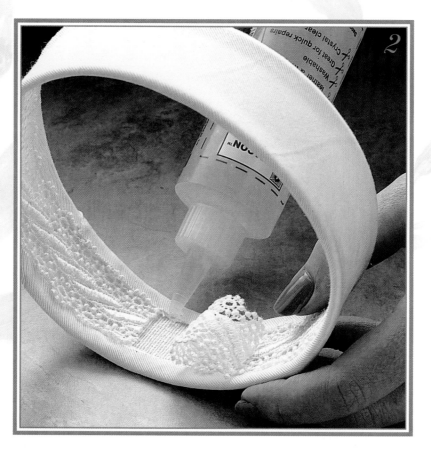

3 Cut length of button looping equal to distance around inside of headpiece; glue to lower inside edge of headpiece, with loops facing top of headpiece. Insert bobby pins in all loops, or, if desired, slide teeth of comb into front loops, inserting bobby pins in rest of loops. If a detachable veil is desired, cut a 5" (12.5 cm) strip of hook and loop tape; glue loop strip to inside, lower center-back edge; hand-stitch hook strip to veil.

4 Embellish headpiece as on page 44, steps 4 and 5.

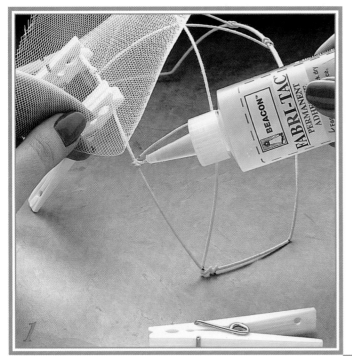

Cut horsehair braid 2" (5 cm) longer than longest side of frame. Glue uncorded edge of horsehair braid to widest outer edge of frame, applying dots of glue to frame. Secure with plastic clothespins, if necessary.

1

2 Pull on gathering cord to shape the horsehair braid to frame. Glue horsehair braid to remaining outer edges. Allow glue to dry. Trim excess horsehair braid even with wire frame at edges.

3 Cover frame with fabric, if desired, as on page 44, steps 1 and 2. Complete headpiece as in steps 3 to 5; cover wire crosspieces with lace first, then fill in remaining areas.

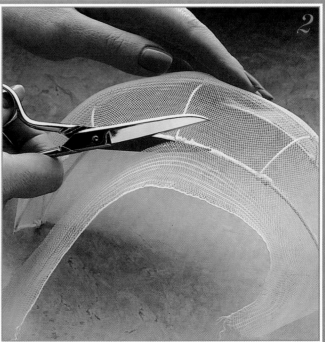

Bridal Party Accessories

Variations
ON THE THEME

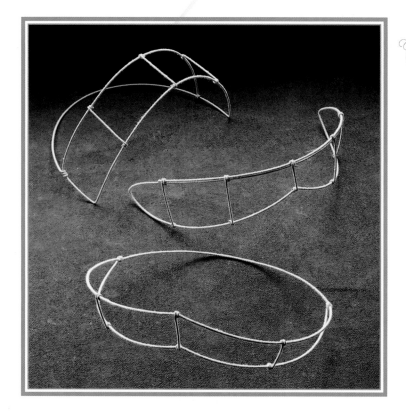

Tip

TO SECURE THE HEADPIECE TO YOUR HAIR, SATURATE STRANDS OF HAIR WITH STYLING GEL AND WIND THEM INTO FLAT PINCURLS AT DESIRED ANCHORING SPOTS ON YOUR HEAD. FOR BOBBY PIN ATTACHMENTS, SLIP BOBBY PIN OVER PINCURL. FOR COMB ATTACHMENTS, WIND A THICKER PINCURL, FLATTEN IT TO YOUR HEAD, AND ANCHOR IT WITH TWO CROSSED BOBBY PINS; WEDGE THE TEETH OF THE COMB DOWN UNDER THE BOBBY PINS.

SATIN & PEARLS

Create a lush arrangement of large satin flowers, available in bridal departments of fabric stores. Add tufts of tulle and pearl sprays. Tuck the back wire under the hair for stability; attach a removable veil beneath the flower band, if desired. (above and opposite, top)

ANTIQUE LACE & BEADS

Cover the frame with ivory Alonçon lace motifs and a cluster of ribbon roses. Accent the motif centers with earth-tone berries, and hand-stitch smaller ribbon roses to the veil in a scattered array. (above and opposite, center)

BEADED LACE

Cover a tiara frame with motifs cut from heavily beaded lace fabric. Attach a veil to the back wire. (above and opposite, bottom)

HAIR *Accessories*

Hair wreaths, barrettes, combs, and headbands can be adorned with fresh, dried, or artificial flowers, ribbons, pearl sprays, and beads. Accessory styles can be adapted for the bride, bridesmaids, or flower girls.

HAIR WREATHS

Grace the head with a lovely wreath made from fresh flowers, silk flowers, or tulle and ribbon rose garland. Prepare a florist wire base to fit so that the wreath will rest in the desired place on the top of the head. If you want to attach a veil to the back of the wreath, make the veil first and determine the base size over the veil.

A fresh flower wreath can be made one or two days before the wedding. Complete steps 1 to 5, on page 52. Then mist the wreath, and store it in a plastic bag in the refrigerator. Complete step 6 just before wearing, to avoid water-spotted or wilted ribbons.

FRESH FLOWER SUGGESTIONS

TYPE	OPTIONS
FLOWER	SWEETHEART (MINIATURE) OR HYBRID (LARGE, STANDARD) ROSES, MINIATURE CARNATIONS, AND CHRYSANTHEMUMS (INCLUDING DAISY AND OTHER VARIETIES)
NOVELTIES	HYPERNIUM BERRIES, ROSE HIPS
GREENS	ITALIAN RUSCUS, PLUMOSA FERN, VARIEGATED ITTOSPORUM, CEDAR, SMILAX, EUONYMUS, EUCALYPTUS, LEATHERLEAF FERN, IVY, CAMELLIA
FILLERS	BABY'S BREATH, LIMONIUM OR CASPIA, STATICE, QUEEN ANNE'S LACE

YOU WILL NEED

- 20-GAUGE FLORIST WIRE
- 24-GAUGE FLORIST WIRE
- WIRE CUTTER
- FLORAL TAPE
- 4 BUTTONHOLE LOOPS

- 20 TO 40 STURDY LONG-LASTING FRESH FLOWERS
- GREENS AND FILLERS
- 3 YD. (2.75 M) SATIN RIBBON, ¼" (6 MM) WIDE

- SMALL WIRED BOW
- HOT GLUE GUN

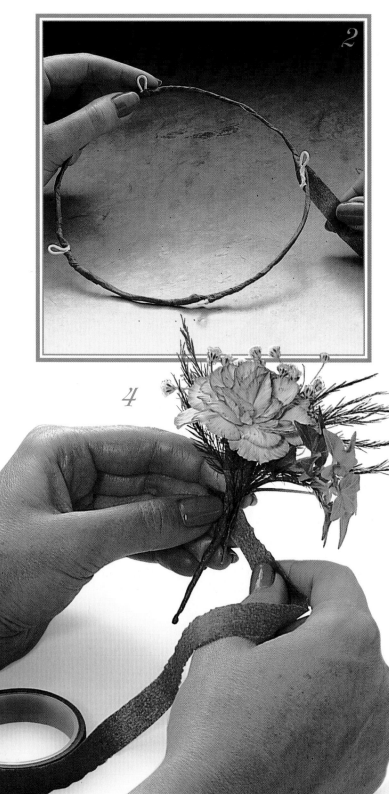

1 Wrap 20-gauge wire three times around in circle of desired size, twisting together slightly, for wreath base. Wrap wire circle with floral tape.

2 Glue four button loops, evenly spaced, to inside of base, for bobby pins; wrap loop ends to base, using floral tape.

3 Wire and tape 20 to 40 flowers as on pages 110 and 111; number of flowers needed depends on desired fullness and size of flowers chosen.

4 Encircle each wired flower back with pieces of filler flower, 1½" to 2" (3.8 to 5 cm) long; join to taped flower stem, using one or two wraps of floral tape. Repeat with greens, forming tight, elliptical cluster.

5 Tape first cluster to base 1" (2.5 cm) from center back; hold flower below head, and tape stem flat onto base. Tape next cluster to base, in same direction, overlapping first cluster by about ½" (1.3 cm), and hiding wire base. Continue around base; avoid covering button loops. Stop taping about 1" (2.5 cm) from first cluster. Trim off extra flower wires, taking care not to cut base.

6 Cut three 1-yd. (0.95 m) lengths of ribbon, for streamers; fold in half. Hang over center back, and glue in place; trim ends to various lengths as desired. Glue wired bow over streamers. Or, in place of streamers and bow, hot-glue veil to inside of center back.

YOU WILL NEED

- 20-GAUGE FLORIST WIRE
- FLORAL TAPE
- WIRE CUTTER
- 4 BUTTONHOLE LOOPS
- HOT GLUE GUN

- SILK FLORAL BRANCHES WITH LEAVES, SUCH AS STEPHANOTIS
- DRIED BABY'S BREATH
- 8 YD. (7.35 M) SATIN RIBBON, 1/4" (6 MM) WIDE

1 Form base, as in steps 1 and 2, opposite.

2 Cut blossoms off floral branches, leaving 1" (2.5 cm) or more stem. Cut leaf clusters into individual leaves, with no stem. Attach one leaf to each blossom stem by putting a dot of glue at base of leaf and wrapping base around stem. Wrap stem and leaf base with floral tape. Prepare about 15 blossoms.

3 Cut small pieces of baby's breath, group together to form clusters, and wrap stems together with floral tape for 1" (2.5 cm). Prepare about 30 clusters.

4 Cut about twenty 4" (10 cm) lengths of ribbon. Bring ends together; wrap with floral tape for 1" (2.5 cm), forming loop.

5 Tape flowers to base as in step 5, opposite. Alternate baby's breath, blossom, baby's breath, ribbon loop.

6 Cut and attach streamers as in step 6, opposite. Fold 1½ yd. (1.4 m) of ribbon into 10 loops, and secure middle of loops with wire; glue loops to base, over streamers. Cut blossoms just below base; glue over center of loops, hiding wire. Or, in place of streamers and bow, hot-glue veil to inside of center back.

Making a Cloud of Roses Wreath

YOU WILL NEED

- 20-GAUGE FLORIST WIRE; WIRE CUTTER
- FLORAL TAPE
- ½ YD. (0.5 M) ILLUSION, 72" (183 CM) WIDE
- ⅛ YD. (0.15 M) POLYFLEECE

- 4 BUTTONHOLE LOOPS
- 2 YD. (1.85 M) RIBBON ROSE GARLAND
- 2 YD. (1.85 M) SATIN RIBBON, 1/16" (1.5 MM) WIDE

- 2 YD. (1.85 M) SATIN RIBBON, ⅛" (3 MM) WIDE
- HOT GLUE GUN

1 Form base as on page 52, step 1. Cut 2" (5 cm) strips of polyfleece, and wrap around circle, gluing in place. Unfold net; scrunch up short width, and wrap around base, overlapping widths. Glue in place.

2 Glue ribbon rose garland to outside of wreath in a zigzag pattern, starting and ending at center back; apply glue under rosebuds, and allow connecting ribbon to form gentle loops.

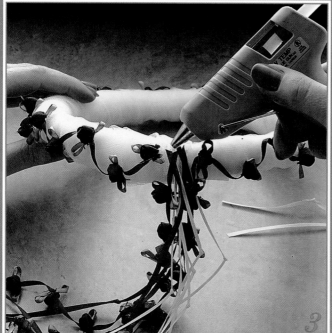

3 Cut two 12" (30.5 cm) streamers of ribbon rose garland, six 14" (35.5 cm) streamers of 1/16" (1.5 mm) ribbon, and two 14" (35.5 cm) streamers of ⅛" (3 mm) ribbon. Tie knots every few inches in streamers without rosebuds. Glue tops of streamers to wreath at center back.

4 Glue cluster of remaining buds over top of streamers. Glue button loops to inside of wreath; attach bobby pins.

Historic Fact

IN EUROPE, BRIDES ONCE WORE WREATHS OF GRAIN OR WHEAT TO ENSURE THAT THEY WOULD HAVE LARGE FAMILIES.

Bridal Party Accessories

BARRETTES & COMBS

Bridesmaids and flower girls can dress up their hair with ribbons and flowers secured to barrettes and combs. Poufing tulle, which comes with a gathering thread sewn through the center, can be used to make an instant ruffle-edged frill for a barrette. By attaching a short veil, brides can wear these accessories, too.

YOU WILL NEED

- LARGE CLIP-TYPE BARRETTE
- BEADING WIRE
- 1 YD (0.95 M) ALENÇON LACE, 3" TO 5" (7.5 TO 12.5 CM) WIDE
- 1½ YD. (1.4 M) POUFING TULLE, 8" (20.5 CM) WIDE
- PEARL SPRAYS
- HOT GLUE GUN

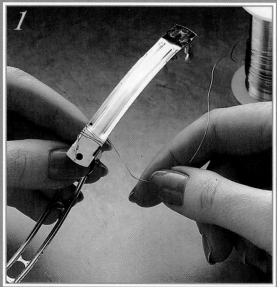

1 Remove tension bar from barrette, and insert wire into hole at barrette end. Twist wire to secure; wind wire over clasp and wrap wire three times around base of barrette, leaving wire attached to spool.

2 Pinch together one end of lace; wrap three times with wire to end of barrette, near clasp. Make loop; pinch together base of loop, and secure to barrette base, wrapping wire three times. Repeat, making four more loops. Secure wire to hole at other end of barrette; trim excess.

3 Tie off gathering threads at one end of poufing tulle. Pull thread to gather until tulle equals the length of bow; tie off. Hand-stitch tulle to underside of bow.

4 Apply small amount of hot glue between loops, for support. Glue pearl sprays between lace loops and between loops and tulle as desired. Replace tension bar.

Making a Ribbon Bow Barrette

YOU WILL NEED

- LARGE CLIP-TYPE BARRETTE
- BEADING WIRE
- 1½ YD. (1.4 M) RIBBON, 1¼" (3.2 CM) WIDE
- 2 YD. (1.85 M) RIBBON, ⅛" (3 MM) WIDE
- 5 RIBBON ROSEBUDS
- PEARL SPRAYS
- LIQUID FRAY PREVENTER
- HOT GLUE GUN

Attach wire to barrette as in step 1, opposite. Wrap ribbon loops to barrette as in step 2, leaving 2½" (6.5 cm) tails at beginning and end. Secure about 11 loops, pointing first loop up, second loop down, and third loop to center; repeat pattern to end of barrette. Secure wire. **1**

Adjust loops evenly along barrette; trim ribbon tails, and apply liquid fray preventer to raw edges. **2**

Cut three 12" (30.5 cm) and two 10" (25.5 cm) streamers from ⅛" (3 mm) ribbon. Hot-glue rosebud to end of each streamer. Hot-glue streamers to underside of bow; glue pearl sprays to base of ribbon loops. **3**

Making a Satin Bow Barrette or Comb

YOU WILL NEED

- ⅛ YD. (0.15 M) SATIN FABRIC
- LARGE CLIP-TYPE BARRETTE OR COMB
- HOT GLUE GUN

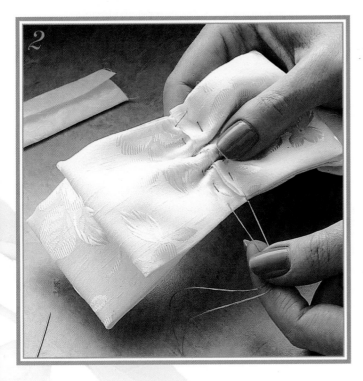

Cut three rectangles from fabric: 6" × 14" (15 × 35.5 cm), 6" × 10" (15 × 25.5 cm), and 2½" × 4½" (6.5 × 11.5 cm). Fold each wider rectangle in half lengthwise, right sides together. Stitch long sides, using ½" (6 mm) seam allowance; leave short ends open. Turn tubes right side out, and press lightly. **1**

Fold ends of each tube to middle; lap slightly, and pin, forming bows. Layer small bow over large bow; hand-baste through all layers ¼" (6 mm) from edges. Pull up on basting thread to gather, and tie off. **2**

Fold under long edges of short rectangle ¾" (2 cm); press. Fold under one short end of folded strip, and wrap strip over center of bows; trim as necessary. Hand-stitch folded edge over raw edge behind bows. **3**

Hot-glue veil to barrette or comb, if desired. Hot-glue bow to barrette or comb. **4**

YOU WILL NEED

- COMB OR BARRETTE
- ¼ YD. (0.25 M) FABRIC
- ABOUT 315 PEARL OR CRYSTAL SEED BEADS
- LIQUID FRAY PREVENTER, OPTIONAL
- BEADING NEEDLE AND THREAD
- HOT GLUE GUN

1 Cut 15 fabric circles, 2¾" (7 cm) in diameter. If fabric tends to ravel, seal edges with liquid fray preventer.

2 Fold circle in half, wrong sides together; do not press. Hand-baste layers together ¼" (6 mm) from raw edge. Pull up gathers tightly, and tie off. Repeat for each circle.

3 Hand-stitch gathered points of five petals together in the center, forming a flower.

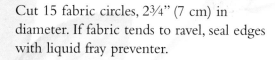

4 Bring threaded beading needle up through middle of flower. String 11 to 13 beads, and insert needle back down near starting point. Sew seven more loops to fill center of flower.

5 Repeat steps 2 to 4 for two more flowers. Hot-glue flowers to comb or barrette.

Historic Fact

COMBS AND BARRETTES FOR THE WEDDING PARTY CAN ALL BE THE SAME OR COORDINATING. IN ANCIENT TIMES, BRIDESMAIDS DRESSED THE SAME AS THE BRIDE TO KEEP EVIL SPIRITS FROM KNOWING WHICH WOMAN WAS TO BE MARRIED.

Bridal Party Accessories

HEADBANDS & CAP

Headbands are a simple way to accessorize young bridesmaids or flower girls. Moiré, taffeta, shantung, satin, and linen make nice coverings for a padded headband that will be embellished with silk ribbon embroidery. For other embellishments, such as ribbon roses, you can either cover the headband in fabric to match the dress or purchase a padded one.

For the reception, kick back a little and exchange the more formal veil for a lighter, fun version, such as a decorated cap, which goes well with the dancing sneakers on page 77. Follow steps 2 to 4, opposite, for fabric flowers, using 5" (12.5 cm) fabric circles and gold beads. Hand-stitch the flowers to the cap, and attach a short veil, if desired.

YOU WILL NEED

- FABRIC
- PLASTIC HEADBAND FORM
- POLYURETHANE FOAM, ¼" TO ½" (6 MM TO 1.3 CM) THICK
- EMBROIDERY HOOP

- ½ YD. (0.5 M) RIBBON OR FLAT TRIM, SLIGHTLY NARROWER THAN HEADBAND
- CHENILLE NEEDLES, SIZES 18 AND 20
- BEADING NEEDLE

- 4 MM AND 7 MM SILK EMBROIDERY RIBBON
- 38 BUGLE BEADS
- 18 GLASS PEARL SEED BEADS
- CRAFT GLUE

1 Spread thin layer of glue on outside of band; secure strip of polyurethane foam. Cut foam even with edges of headband. If using ½" (1.3 cm) foam, trim foam ½" (1.3 cm) shorter than ends. Clamp ends of foam with clothespins until glue dries.

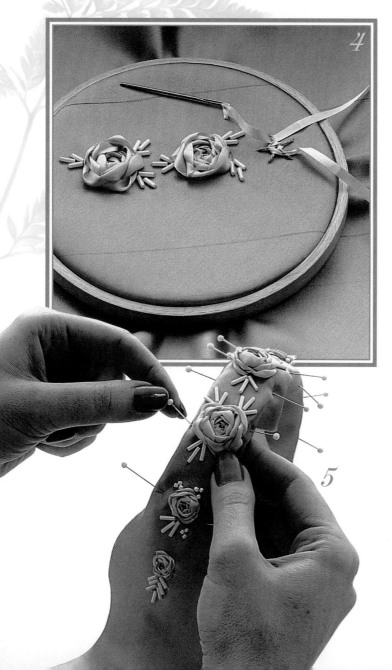

2 Mark 3" × 23" (7.5 × 58.5 cm) rectangle on bias of fabric. Secure fabric in embroidery hoop.

3 Embroider two 1" (2.5 cm) spiderweb roses (page 75) in center of strip, using size 18 chenille needle and 7 mm silk embroidery ribbon. With beading needle and double strand of thread, stitch three groups of three bugle beads around each rose; stitch through each bead twice.

4 Embroider remaining roses, using size 20 chenille needle and 4 mm silk embroidery ribbon. To left and right of center roses, embroider ¾" (2 cm) spiderweb rose; stitch a group of three bugle beads and three groups of three seed beads around each rose. Embroider ½" (1.3 cm) spiderweb rose next to each ¾" (2 cm) rose. Stitch seven bugle beads in a chevron pattern to finish off design.

5 Remove fabric from hoop; cut out rectangle. Center rectangle on headband; hold in place with straight pins. Trim fabric so edges extend one-half the width of the headband; round ends about ⅜" (1 cm) beyond headband. Clip fabric at ends, and glue to inside of headband.

6 Glue one long edge of fabric to inside of headband, applying glue to headband; work in sections, keeping fabric smooth. Repeat for opposite side. Remove pins.

7 Glue ribbon or flat trim over raw edges on inside of headband; turn under ends. If veil will be used, attach as on page 31, step 4.

YOU WILL NEED

- PURCHASED PADDED HEADBAND
- 72" (183 CM) OF SATIN RIBBON, ⅜" OR ½" (1 OR 1.3 CM) WIDE, FOR 6 ROSES
- 15" (38 CM) SATIN RIBBON, ⅜" (1 CM) WIDE, FOR LEAVES
- HOT GLUE GUN

1 Cut ribbon into six 12" (30.5 cm) lengths, for roses. Cut ribbon into six 2½" (6.5 cm) lengths, for leaves.

2 Fold rose ribbon under diagonally at center, forming right angle. Turn the end that is underneath back over the center. Repeat with other end. Continue folding alternate ends back over previous folds, forming square stack. Stop when ends are 1" (2.5 cm) long.

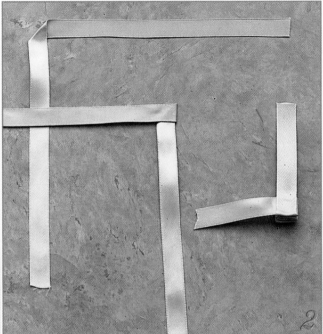

3 Turn stack over. Hold only the two ends, and release the stack. Holding ends securely, but loosely enough so they can slide, pull one end gently. A rose will form. Stop pulling when the excess ribbon is pulled out and the center of the rose sinks in.

4 Hand-stitch through the back of the rose to hold all layers firmly in place. Trim off the ribbon ends.

5 Fold each leaf ribbon into two loops; hand-stitch to back of roses.

6 Make five more roses. Hot-glue roses to headband, spaced evenly. If veil will be used, attach as on page 31, step 4.

Tip

TWO MONTHS BEFORE THE WEDDING, USE A DEEP HAIR CONDITIONER WEEKLY. YOUR HAIR WILL FEEL BETTER AND BE EASIER TO CONTROL.

BRIDAL
Garters

*Garters are quick, fun, and easy to sew.
They can be delicate or bold, usually
reflecting the style of the dress.*

Sew a fabric garter edged with lace, or make a garter from a
width of galloon lace, which has two decorative edges. Either
style can be embellished with ribbons, lace appliqués, ribbon
flowers, beads, and other trims.

Consider making two garters for your wedding day; one for
your own keepsake and one for the ritual toss.

Making a Fabric Garter

YOU WILL NEED

- ¼ YD. (0.25 M) FABRIC
- 1 YD. (0.95 M) GALLOON LACE, FOR EDGING
- ELASTIC, ½" (1.3 CM) WIDE
- SATIN RIBBON, ¼" (6 MM) WIDE
- SMALL SAFETY PIN OR BODKIN
- FABRIC GLUE

1

1 Cut fabric strip 5" (12.5 cm) wide with
length equal to one-and-one-half to two
times leg measurement. (Fullness depends
on thickness of fabric.) Zigzag or serge
upper edge; fold under 1" (2.5 cm), and
press. Stitch close to fold and agaim ¾"
(2 cm) below first row of stitching,
forming casing.

Continued

2 Lap lace over lower edge of fabric strip, right sides up; stitch along upper scallop of lace, using zigzag. Trim away fabric behind lace, about ⅛" (3 mm) from the stitching.

3 Cut elastic 1" (2.5 cm) larger than leg measurement. Attach bodkin or safety pin to one end of elastic; thread elastic though casing. Anchor other end of elastic inside casing with stitching line, ¼" (6 mm) from fabric edge.

4 Wrap garter around leg, and adjust snugness of elastic as desired; trim away any excess elastic even with casing opening, and pin.

5 Align ends, right sides together; pin. Serge ¼" (6 mm) from edge, or use straight stitch and finish edges together with zigzag stitch.

6 Tie ribbon into bow, and glue to lower edge of casing at center front, or hand-stitch bow, being careful not to catch elastic inside casing. Embellish as desired.

YOU WILL NEED

- GALLOON LACE, ABOUT 5" (12.5 CM) WIDE
- SATIN RIBBON, ¾" (2 CM) WIDE
- ELASTIC, ½" (1.3 CM) WIDE
- SMALL SAFETY PIN OR BODKIN
- FABRIC GLUE

1 Cut lace and satin ribbon two times leg measurement. Pin ribbon to right side of lace, 1" (2.5 cm) below upper edge; stitch along upper and lower edges of ribbon, leaving ends open, for casing.

2 Follow steps 3 to 5, opposite. Cut 20" (51 cm) of satin ribbon, and tie into bow; notch tails. Glue bow over casing at center front, or hand-stitch bow, being careful not to catch elastic inside casing. Embellish as desired.

Variations

ON THE THEME

LACE GARTER WITH BEADED DANGLES

Attach hand-beaded dangles behind the bow on a lace garter. For each dangle, knot the thread and take a stitch in the lower edge of the casing. Slip the needle through several beads, ending with a seed bead. Bring the needle back through all beads except the seed bead, then stitch to casing edge. Secure threads on the wrong side after each dangle.

ROSES & PEARLS

Serge the lower edge of a satin garter, then apply narrow beaded trim. Glue or hand-stitch ribbon roses over the casing; embellish them with pearl loops.

BLUE SHEER RIBBON

Make a garter from wide sheer ribbon with a satin ribbon casing and bow. Stitch "something old", such as a cameo pendant, to the center of the bow. Or, if you intend to toss the garter, select an inexpensive charm.

LACE APPLIQUÉS

Hand-stitch lace appliqués to a satin garter. Trim the bottom with picot lace edging.

Shoes

Beads, lace, and ribbon can transform plain pumps or ballet slippers into one-of-a-kind footwear for the bride and her attendants.

Such trims can also be used to change tennis shoes into dancing shoes for the reception. Most embellishments can be attached with hot glue or a fabric glue; choose one that will dry clear and flexible. When sewing beads directly to shoes, choose a fine but sturdy sewing needle, rather than a beading needle. A spray sealer or stain repellent can be applied to the finished shoes, if desired.

Historic Fact

IN OLD BRITAIN, THE FATHER GAVE HIS NEW SON-IN-LAW ONE OF THE BRIDE'S SHOES. SHE WAS TAPPED ON THE HEAD WITH IT, AS A SIGN OF HER HUSBAND'S AUTHORITY. HE, IN TURN, HAD TO PROMISE TO BE GOOD TO HER.

Accenting Shoes with Pearls

YOU WILL NEED

- SATIN PUMPS OR BALLET SLIPPERS
- 56 OBLONG PEARL BEADS, 3 × 6 MM
- 322 ROUND PEARL BEADS, 3 MM
- FINE SEWING NEEDLE (NOT A BEADING NEEDLE)
- BEADING THREAD

1 Mark center front on shoe opening with pin. Bring threaded needle up from inside to outside of shoe, at point 3" (7.5 cm) from center front.

2 String 28 oblong beads. Lay string of beads along upper edge, to a point on opposite side; there should be 14 beads on each side of center front. Insert needle down through shoe where beads end.

3 Bring needle up between last two beads, below bead thread; insert needle back down above bead thread. Repeat to end, anchoring every other bead.

4 Bring needle up again at starting point; string 15 round beads. Insert needle back down through shoe at point four oblong beads away, forming loose-hanging scallop of beads. Bring needle up, close to previous stitch; repeat to end, making seven scallops. Tie off thread.

5 Bring needle up at one starting point of center scallop; string 15 round beads. Insert needle back down near starting point, making small loop.

6 Bring needle back up at same point; string 26 round beads. Insert needle down at opposite end of center scallop, making larger scallop. Make small loop, as in step 5, above.

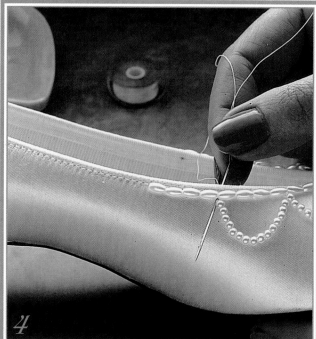

Adorning Shoes with Silk Ribbon Embroidery

YOU WILL NEED

- SATIN PUMPS OR BALLET SLIPPERS
- SILK RIBBON IN DESIRED COLORS, 7 MM FOR FLOWERS, 4 MM FOR

LEAVES AND STEMS
- CRYSTAL OR PEARL SEED BEADS
- CHENILLE NEEDLE, SIZE 20 OR 22
- BEADING NEEDLE

- BEADING THREAD
- WHITE, MEDIUMWEIGHT WOVEN INTERFACING
- FABRIC GLUE

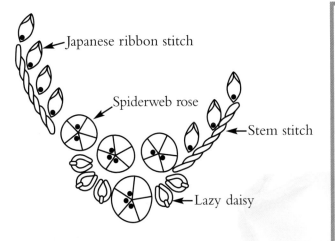

Japanese ribbon stitch

Spiderweb rose

Stem stitch

Lazy daisy

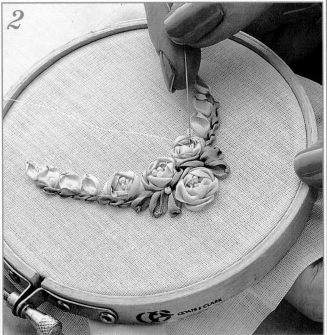

1 Enlarge design as necessary; transfer onto interfacing, for right shoe; transfer mirror image for left shoe. Secure interfacing in embroidery hoop.

Embroider designs, using chenille needle, as on pages 72 to 75. Stitch beads into place, using beading needle and beading thread.

Cut out embroidered designs carefully, leaving scant margin of interfacing.

Spread thin layer of glue onto backs of embroidered designs; secure designs on toes of shoes, with longer side of design on outside of each shoe. Allow to dry.

2

3

4

MARKING DESIGN

Transfer design to fabric using light pencil or water-soluble marking pen.

PREPARING FABRIC

Keep fabric taut in an embroidery hoop. If fabric doesn't fit hoop, place fabric over a support fabric, and stitch together along edge of design; cut away support fabric under design before embroidering. Remove design fabric from support fabric when stitching is completed.

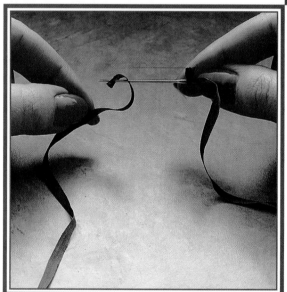

THREADING & KNOTTING

Thread 18" (46 cm) length of ribbon through eye of chenille needle, size 18 to 20; the higher the number, the finer the needle. Pierce ribbon ½" (1.3 cm) from threaded end; pull ribbon through, locking tail on needle eye. Fold over opposite end ¼" (6 mm), and pierce center of both layers with needle. Holding folded end, draw needle and ribbon through to form a soft knot at end of ribbon.

ENDING

End the ribbon by running needle under a few stitches on back side of fabric; pierce ribbon of a nearby stitch, if desired, but do not disturb design on right side. Trim off ribbon tail.

JAPANESE RIBBON STITCH

Bring needle up from underside. Smooth ribbon flat in direction of stitch (arrow). Insert needle at end of stitch, piercing center of ribbon. Pull needle through to underside until ribbon curls at tip; take care not to pull ribbon too tight.

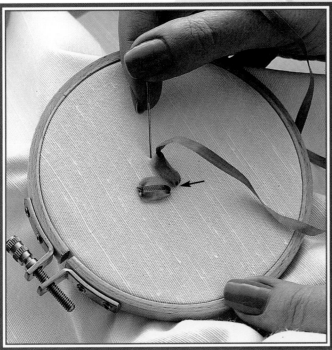

LAZY DAISY STITCH

Bring needle up from underside at "petal" base; insert needle right next to exit point (arrow), and bring needle back up at "petal" tip. Pull ribbon through fabric, forming small, smooth loop. Pass needle through loop; secure with small straight stitch at "petal" tip.

LOOP STITCH

Bring needle up from underside; pull ribbon through. Loop ribbon smoothly over index finger opposite needle hand. Insert needle into fabric right in front of exit point. Pull ribbon through fabric until loop is desired size, removing finger as ribbon tightens. Hold completed loop as you begin the next stitch.

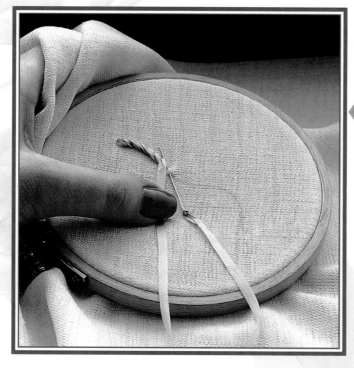

STEM STITCH

Bring needle up through fabric at start of marked or imaginary line; make small straight stitch. Bring needle back through fabric part-way back and alongside previous stitch. Repeat continuously for desired length; keep ribbon smooth without twisting.

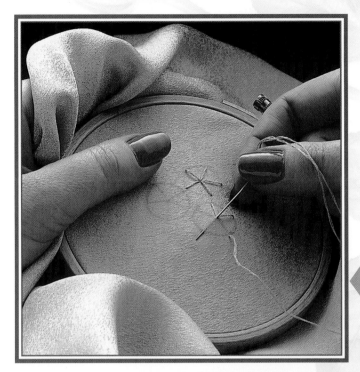

SPIDERWEB ROSE

Draw a circle with five evenly spaced "spokes." Using embroidery floss, form a stitch along each of the spokes, and tie off.

Bring ribbon up at center of web; weave over and under the first two spokes, and gently pull the ribbon through, forming the first "petal." Continue weaving ribbon over and under the spokes in a circular fashion, working gradually outward, until spokes are covered and desired fullness is achieved. Keep ribbon loose; twists in ribbon add interest. Push needle through to back, making final "petal."

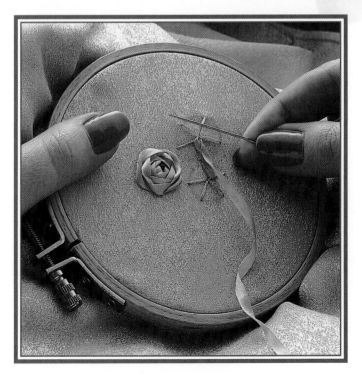

Variations
ON THE THEME

RIBBON BOWS

Cut narrow wired ribbon into two sets of strips: 16", 12", and 2" (40.5, 30.5, and 5 cm) long. For each shoe, form 16" (40.5 cm) strip into four loops; lay 12" (30.5 cm) strip behind loops for tails. Wrap 2" (5 cm) piece around center of loops and tails; overlap ends behind bow, and hot-glue together. Hot-glue bow to shoe toe. Arrange and glue tails along shoe sides.

LACE-COVERED SHOES

Cut Alençon lace fabric into small motifs. Glue motifs onto shoe, using fabric glue; center larger designs over toe and work toward heel. Cover entire surface uniformly. Secure all edges with glue.

DANCING SNEAKERS

Trim design lines of leather or canvas sport shoes with decorative cording. Replace shoelaces with wide white ribbon; roll and glue ends as shown. Glue ribbon bows to heels, and accent with ribbon roses.

LACE & PEARLS

Apply fabric glue liberally to the wrong side of lace appliqués; apply to front and outer sides of shoes. Accent design details with pearls.

SHOE CLIPS

Secure ribbon bows and pearl sprays to removable shoe clips, using hot glue. Cut shanks off heart buttons, using wire cutter, and glue over bows.

Gloves

Gloves add an elegant touch to your attire. They come in satin, crushed velvet, sheer organdy, and lace, and can be easily embellished with trims.

Generally, wear short gloves with a long-sleeved gown; wear long gloves with a short-sleeved or sleeveless gown. Because gloves stretch and are handled a lot, attach trims by sewing rather than by gluing.

Accent gloves with trims that reflect the style of the gown; perhaps repeat an embellishment used in the headpiece. For instance, hand-stitch a smaller version of the satin bow (page 57) to the back of the wrist, echoing a bow used in a barrette or pillbox hat. Look for ribbon trims that match the gloves, such as the deep lavender ruched ribbon on the glove at right. Sew the trim loosely along the cuffs, allowing room for the gloves to stretch when worn. Continue down the outside seam to just below the finger. Customize plain gloves with a silk ribbon embroidery and bead design, following the tips and stitch directions on pages 72 to 75. Or stitch purchased ribbon roses along the cuffs of simple floral lace gloves, and stitch pearl beads to the centers of the flower motifs. Sew through each bead twice, for added security.

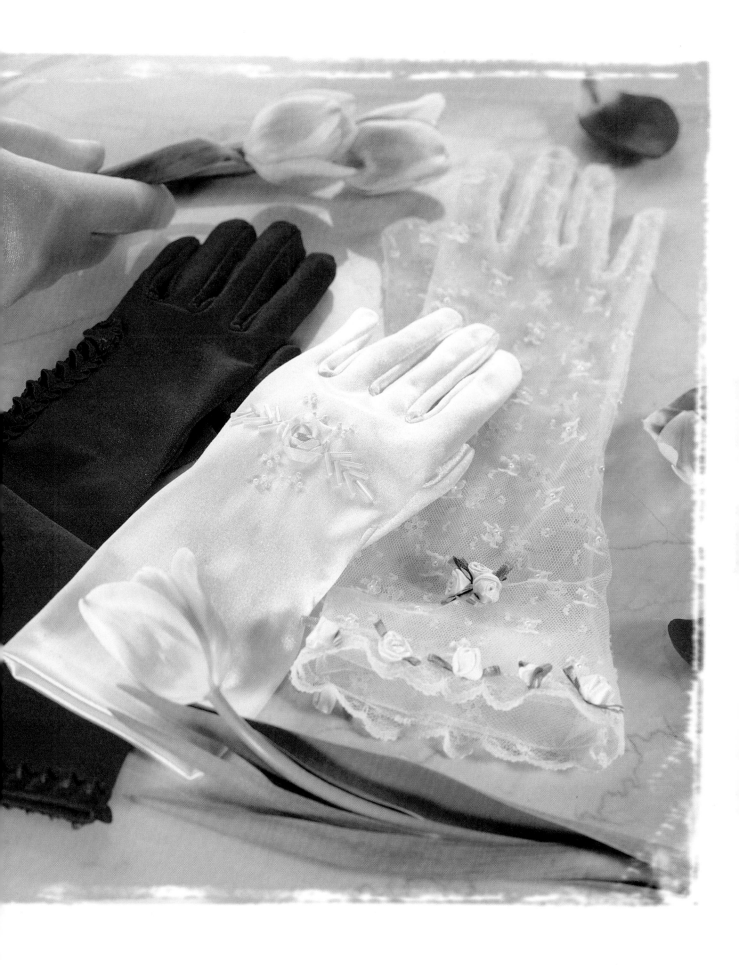

DRAWSTRING *Bag*

*A drawstring fabric bag
for the bride or bridesmaids is a
perfect catchall for the occasion.*

Make the bag from mediumweight fabric, such as taffeta, brocade, velvet, velveteen, moiré taffeta, or satin. Embellish the bag with ribbon roses (page 118), fabric flowers (page 58), or whatever suits your fancy.

The bag top and casing edges can be serge-finished for a decorative effect. Or, the bag can be sewn completely with a conventional sewing machine.

Tip

AFTER THE WEDDING, USE YOUR DRAWSTRING BAG TO STORE SMALL REMEMBRANCES OF THE DAY, SUCH AS TABLE FAVORS, GARTER, INVITATION, AND FLOWER PETALS.

YOU WILL NEED

- ³⁄₈ YD. (0.35 M) OUTER FABRIC
- ³⁄₈ YD. (0.35 M) LINING FABRIC
- 1½ YD. (1.4 M) NARROW DECORATIVE CORDING OR FILLED SATIN CORDING, FOR DRAWSTRINGS
- PLASTIC CANVAS
- DECORATIVE RAYON THREAD, FOR SERGED EDGES

1 Cut one 11" × 21" (28 × 53.5 cm) rectangle from outer fabric; mark a line on right side of fabric 2" (5 cm) from upper long edge. Cut two 1" × 11" (2.5 × 28 cm) casing strips from lining or outer fabric, if the edges will be serged; cut the strips 2" × 11" (5 × 28 cm) if edges will be folded under. Cut one 12½" × 21" (31.8 × 53.5 cm) rectangle from lining. Cut 4¼" (10.8 cm) circles from outer fabric and lining. Cut 3¼" (8.2 cm) circle from plastic canvas.

2 Serge long edges of casing strips, using overlock or rolled hem stitch; use decorative rayon thread in loopers and regular thread in the needle. Stitch ¼" (6 mm) double-fold hems at short ends. Or, if using conventional machine, stitch double-fold hem on short edges, and press long edges under ½" (1.3 cm).

3 Pin casing strips to outer fabric, with top edge of strip along marked line and outer hemmed ends ½" (1.3 cm) from sides; inner hemmed ends meet at center. Stitch close to long edges of casing strips; leave ends open.

4   Fold rectangle, right sides together, matching short ends; stitch ½" (1.3 cm) seam, taking care not to catch casings in seam. Press open.

5   Stitch two rows of gathering stitches ⅜" and ½" (1 and 1.3 cm) from lower edge; pin-mark lower edge and circle from outer fabric into fourths. Pin circle to lower edge, right sides together, matching pin marks; pull gathering threads to distribute fullness evenly. Stitch ½" (1.3 cm) seam; stitch again close to previous stitches.

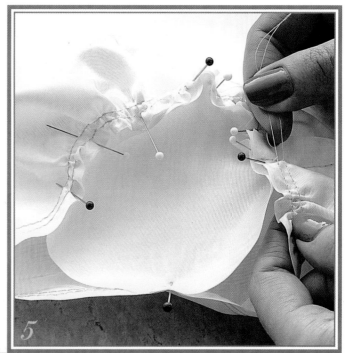

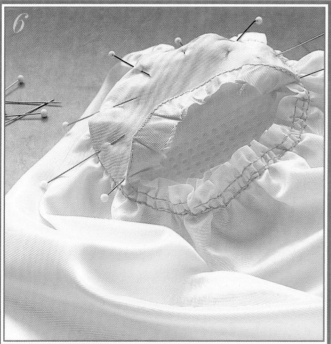

Stitch ½" (1.3 cm) from edge of lining circle; press seam allowance under along stitching line. Place plastic canvas circle on bottom of bag, inside seam allowance. Pin lining circle, wrong side down, over plastic canvas; slipstitch in place.

Fold lining fabric in half crosswise, right sides together; stitch ½" (1.3 cm) seam on side and bottom. If top edge of fabric and lining will be encased instead of serge-stitched, leave a 6" (15 cm) opening on bottom for turning.

Continued

6

7

9

8 For a serged top, pin top edge of lining to top edge of purse, wrong sides together. Serge edge with overlock stitch. Or, for seam-encased edge, pin top edge of lining to top edge of purse, right sides together. Stitch ½" (1.3 cm) seam. Turn purse right side out through opening in lining; stitch opening closed, and tuck lining into purse. Press upper edge of purse, and edgestitch.

9 Cut cording into two 26" (66 cm) lengths, for drawstrings. Using bodkin or safety pin, feed one cord through casings, all around bag, beginning and ending at one side. Repeat for remaining cord, beginning and ending at opposite side. Knot ends of each cord; knot cord ends together for carrying. Draw cords to close bag.

10 Make three ribbon roses as on page 118, steps 1 to 5. Hand-stitch to center front, under casing. Attach other embellishments as desired.

Variations
ON THE THEME

SILK RIBBON EMBROIDERY
Before constructing bag, embellish outer fabric with silk ribbon embroidery and beads. Copy the design shown here, or create your own, using the stitches on pages 72 to 75. Wrap cord ends with thread to prevent fraying.

LACE OVER SATIN
Use colored lining to accent lace pattern. Add an heirloom button. Seal cord ends with liquid fray preventer; stitch together and hide inside casing.

MONOGRAMMED VELVET
Secure purchased monogram to bag before sewing. Stitch beaded design around monogram for added detail. Adorn with a fabric bow (page 57).

CEREMONY ACCENTS

Like theater props, items carried or used to decorate the ceremony play an important supporting role. While conveying the wedding theme, they add charm, style, and richness.

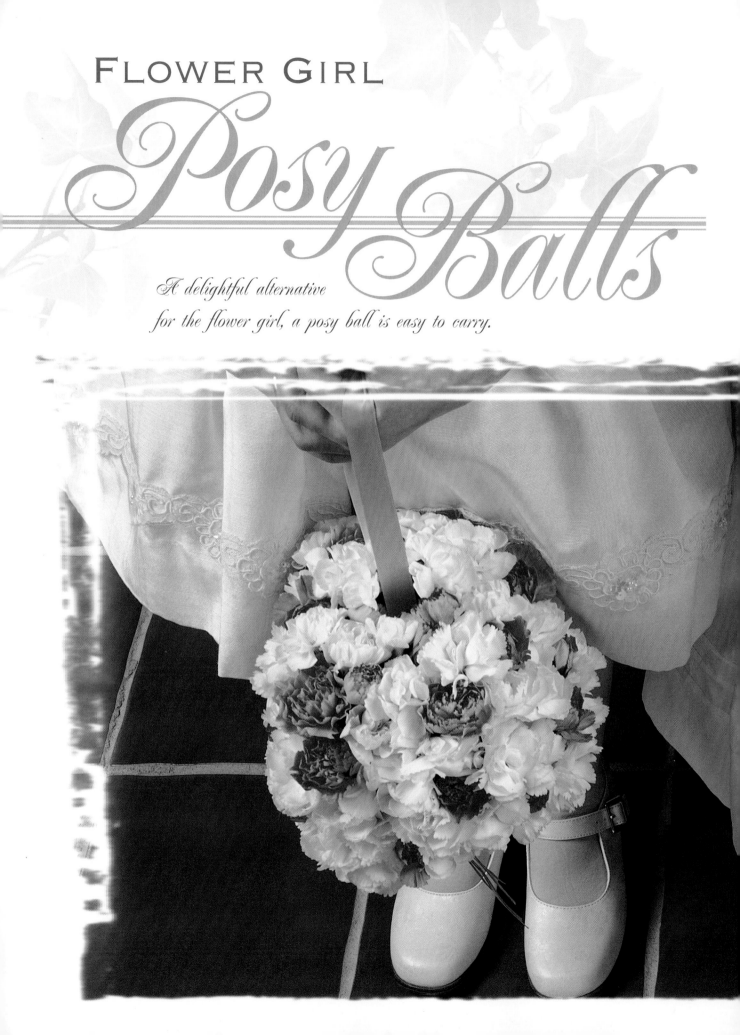

FLOWER GIRL
Posy Balls

A delightful alternative
for the flower girl, a posy ball is easy to carry.

Constructed from fresh, artificial, or dried flowers, posy balls have a charm all their own. The size can be adjusted to suit the age of the flower girl.

Make the fresh-flower posy ball up to 48 hours ahead, using resilient flowers such as miniature carnations. Or substitute artificial flowers and greens, following the same directions.

Start the twig ball at least two weeks before the wedding, allowing enough time for the flowers to dry completely.

Select the lace ball with silk roses for a very young flower girl. It is lightest in weight and can be jostled about with little concern for its durability.

YOU WILL NEED

- STYROFOAM® BALL, 2" TO 4" (5 TO 10 CM) IN DIAMETER
- 20 TO 50 FRESH MINIATURE CARNATIONS OR ARTIFICIAL FLOWERS
- FRESH GREEN LEAVES OR ARTIFICIAL GREENS

- 1 YD. (0.95 M) RIBBON, ⅝" (1.5 CM) WIDE
- ⅔ YD. (0.63 M) RIBBON, ¼" (6 MM) WIDE
- FLAT-HEADED STRAIGHT PINS
- HOT GLUE GUN

1 Cut two pieces of ⅝" (1.5 cm) ribbon equal in length to circumference of Styrofoam ball plus 1" (2.5 cm). Make loop with one ribbon, overlapping ends ½" (1.3 cm); hot-glue. Glue loop to top of ball, and secure with two straight pins.

2 Wrap second ribbon around ball, crossing through top loop. Overlap ends at bottom of ball. Hot-glue ends together and to ball; secure with two straight pins.

3 Hot-glue fresh or artificial leaves flat to ball, covering surface.

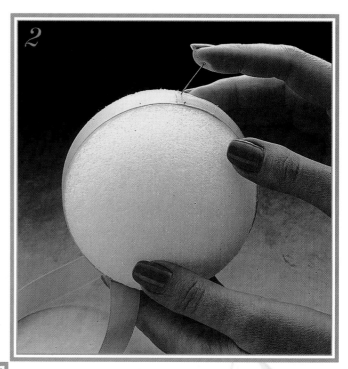

4 Cut flower heads off stems, just below calyx. Starting next to ribbon, hot-glue flowers onto ball, overlapping slightly so ball doesn't show. Cover half the ball. If using fresh carnations, hang ball by loop to finish other side. Glue flowers over area where top ribbon loop is attached. Omit step 5 if using artificial flowers.

5 Mist inside of plastic bag. Insert several toothpicks all around ball, between flowers. Insert ball into bag, and seal. Prop ball up by toothpicks to avoid flattening flowers. Store in refrigerator.

6 Before use, cut five lengths of ¼" (6 mm) ribbon, 3" to 5" (7.5 to 12.5 cm) long. Hot-glue ends to bottom of ball, and secure with straight pins.

Making a Twig Ball

YOU WILL NEED

- 6" (15 CM) TWIG BALL
- 8 TO 12 FRESH, FRAGRANT FLOWERS
- POTPOURRI OIL

- 5 YD. (4.6 M) RIBBON, 5/8" (1.5 CM) WIDE
- 1 YD. (0.95 M) RIBBON, 1/4" (6 MM) WIDE, FOR STREAMERS

- SMALL CLUSTER ARTIFICIAL FLOWERS AND GREENS
- 24-GAUGE FLORIST WIRE
- HOT GLUE GUN

1 Start project two weeks before wedding. Cut off heads of fragrant flowers; insert through openings of ball. Gently shake and turn ball once a day to ensure proper drying of flowers.

2 Wrap 6" (15 cm) length of wire around crossed twigs on top of ball; twist to secure, leaving tails.

3 Cut four lengths of 1/8" (1.5 cm) ribbon, equal in length to circumference of ball plus 1" (2.5 cm). Wrap one ribbon around ball; twist wire tails around ends to secure. Repeat for two more ribbons, spacing them evenly. Trim ends of wire and ribbons. Secure intersections at top and bottom, using hot glue.

4 Make loop with remaining ribbon, overlapping ends 1/2" (1.3 cm); hot-glue. Secure loop to top of ball, using wire. Glue cluster of artificial flowers and greens over joined area.

5 Cut three lengths of 1/4" (6 mm) ribbon, 12" (30.5 cm) long, for streamers. Layer and fold in half. Slip fold loop under crossed ribbons at bottom of ball; insert loose ends through loop, and pull snug. Trim streamer ends to various lengths. Add few drops of potpourri oil for fragrance, if desired.

YOU WILL NEED

- 3" (7.5 CM) STYROFOAM® BALL
- 3½" YD. (3.2 M) PREGATHERED LACE, 1¼" (3.2 CM) WIDE
- 2¼ YD. (2.1 M) SATIN RIBBON, ⅛" (3 MM) WIDE
- 12 SILK ROSES, 1" (2.5 CM) IN DIAMETER
- 6 SPRAYS OF LILY OF THE VALLEY WITH PEARLS
- 26-GAUGE CRAFT WIRE
- SHARP, POINTED METAL NAIL FILE
- HOT GLUE GUN

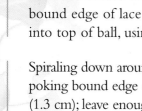

1 Roll end of lace into tight circle. Poke bound edge of lace circle ½" (1.3 cm) deep into top of ball, using point of nail file.

2 Spiraling down around the ball, continue poking bound edge of lace into ball every ½" (1.3 cm); leave enough slack in lace between pokes to allow binding to lie flat on surface. Cover entire ball, allowing ¼" (6 mm) space between rows.

3 Cut excess lace at bottom, leaving short tail. Roll tail into small circle, as in step 1; poke into ball.

4 Cut a 10" (25.5 cm) piece of ribbon, form a loop, and hot-glue ends to center of top of ball. Hot-glue two roses to base of loop.

5 Cut two pieces of ribbon, 11" and 25" (28 and 63.5 cm) long. Fold long piece into six loops, leaving 5" (12.5 cm) tails. Center short ribbon over loops; secure at center with wire. Twist wire ends together and insert wire into center of circle at bottom of ball. Repeat for circle at top of ball, cutting short ribbon 9" (23 cm) long.

6 Hot-glue one end of lily of the valley sprays to center of circle at bottom of ball. Hot-glue remaining roses into lace, evenly spacing them around ball.

Baskets

A hand-trimmed flower basket will charm the flower girl and everyone watching her carry it up the aisle.

Cover a basket in fabric to coordinate with the bridal party. Or, simply run ribbon through wide lace beading, and secure it to the basket edge. Baskets can be filled with fresh, dried, or artificial flower petals, potpourri, or confetti for the flower girl to strew down the aisle. As an alternative to a bouquet, the flower girl can carry a basket filled with a fresh flower arrangement. While adding an adorable touch to the ceremony, the basket is also a memorable keepsake for her.

Tip

IF YOUR FLOWER GIRL WILL BE SPRINKLING PETALS DOWN THE AISLE, KEEP AN EXTRA BAG OF PETALS HANDY IN CASE OF ACCIDENTAL SPILLS.

Covering a Basket with Fabric

YOU WILL NEED

- BASKET WITH FLARED RIM AND HANDLE
- FABRIC
- 1 TO 2 YD. (0.95 TO 1.85 M) EACH OF TWO COORDINATING RIBBONS
- POLYESTER BATTING
- HOT GLUE GUN

1 Measure basket from inside base up over rim, down the side and across bottom, up opposite side, and over rim to inside base. Cut fabric circle 2" (5 cm) wider than this measurement.

2 Place basket upside down over tall bottle. Secure center of fabric circle to base, using hot glue. Wrap fabric down sides and over the rim.

3 Tie string tightly around basket. Pleat out fabric fullness evenly. Glue ribbon tightly around basket just below rim, turning under one end and overlapping the other.

4 Cut slit from fabric edge to handle base on each side. Turn basket over; work fabric around handles and pleat out fullness down into pocket. Apply bead of hot glue around base of basket pocket; secure fabric.

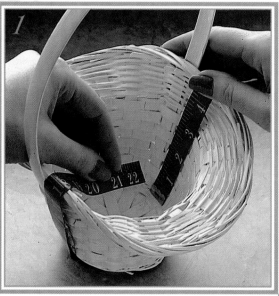

5 Cut cardboard to fit loosely inside bottom of basket; cut matching piece of batting. Cut fabric 1" (2.5 cm) larger than cardboard. Hot-glue batting to cardboard.

6 Center cardboard, batting side down, over wrong side of fabric. Wrap fabric to back; glue in place. Secure padded cardboard to inside basket base, using hot glue.

7 Knot ribbon around one base of handle. Angle and wrap ribbon around handle to opposite base; knot and trim. Tie ribbon bow to each handle base, covering knots.

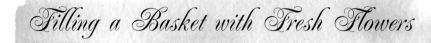

Filling a Basket with Fresh Flowers

YOU WILL NEED

- BASKET WITH HANDLE, EMBELLISHED AS DESIRED
- FLORAL FOAM FOR FRESH FLOWERS
- PLASTIC CONTAINER OR STURDY PLASTIC BAG TO FIT INTO BASKET
- FLORAL ADHESIVE CLAY
- SHREDDED PAPER OR SPANISH MOSS, OPTIONAL
- FLOWERS AND GREENS WITH STEMS; SINGLE VARIETY OR UP TO THREE DIFFERENT KINDS
- EMBELLISHMENTS, SUCH AS RIBBON OR BEAD SPRAYS

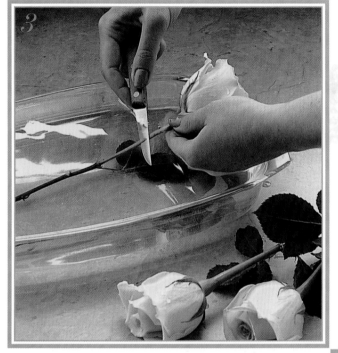

1 Place plastic container or bag into pocket of basket; secure with floral adhesive clay. Surround container with shredded paper or Spanish moss, if desired.

2 Cut fresh floral foam slightly larger and about ¾" (2 cm) higher than container. Soak in water until saturated, allowing water to soak in from bottom and sides, but not top, thereby preventing air pockets that could cause wilted flowers.

3 Place foam into container or plastic bag. Cut flower stems at an angle to desired heights while submerging them in water. Remove any leaves that will be covered by foam.

4 Insert flowers into foam, spacing evenly around container and varying heights as desired. Fill in with greens.

5 Insert other embellishments as desired, such as ribbon or bead sprays.

RING BEARER
Pillows

Send the ring bearer up the aisle with a special pillow holding the rings.

Sew a lace patchwork pillow, using various widths and styles of ribbons and laces. If you prefer, sew a romantic heart-shaped pillow in satin, shantung, or moiré, embellished with silk ribbon embroidery. Or create an organdy potpourri-filled flange pillow that will emit a soft floral scent. Each pillow has a ribbon handle on the underside for easy carrying. A ribbon sewn to the pillow top secures the wedding rings or symbolic replicas.

Making a Ribbon and Lace Patchwork Pillow

YOU WILL NEED

- WATER-SOLUBLE STABILIZER, 6" X 24" (15 X 61 CM)
- ⅔ YD. (0.63 M) EACH OF FOUR TO SIX RIBBONS AND LACES WHOSE COMBINED WIDTH EQUALS ABOUT 5¾" (14.5 CM)
- 11" (28 CM) SQUARE COLORED FABRIC, FOR FRONT UNDERLAY
- ¾ YD. (0.7 M) SATIN RIBBON, ⅛" (3 MM) WIDE, FOR RING TIE
- ¾ YD. (0.7 M) FABRIC, FOR RUFFLE AND PILLOW BACK
- 11" (28 CM) SATIN RIBBON, ½" (1.3 CM) WIDE, FOR HANDLE
- 10" (25.5 CM) PILLOW FORM OR POLYESTER FIBERFILL

1   Arrange ribbons and laces side by side on stabilizer, butting or overlapping long edges as necessary for a total width of about 5¾" (14.5 cm). For best results, plan a trim at least 1½" (3.8 cm) wide at outer edge and an opaque trim at inner edge. Pin in place.

2   Zigzag over long edges through stabilizer, joining ribbons and laces into solid strip.

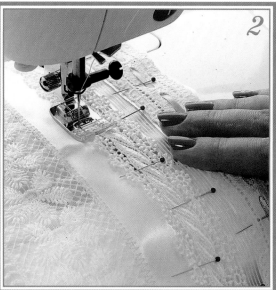

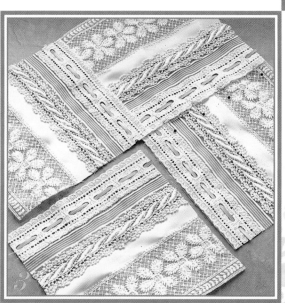

Cut strip into four 5¾" (14.5 cm) squares. Lay out squares so upper left and lower right trims run vertically and opaque edges are toward center; position upper right and lower left squares so trims run horizontally and opaque edges are toward center.   *3*

Lap solid edge of upper left square ¼" (6 mm) over pieced edge of upper right square; zigzag together. Continue zigzagging squares together, in clockwise direction, overlapping edges with solid edge on top. When joining last square, clip as necessary to allow center to lie flat.   *4*

5   Rinse away stabilizer, following the manufacturer's directions. Iron patchwork dry, using low setting.

6   Pin patchwork over underlay, right sides up; baste scant ½" (1.3 cm) from edges. Stitch center of ring tie to center of patchwork.

7   Cut two ruffle strips 7" × 44" (18 × 112 cm). Stitch short ends, right sides together, forming circle. Fold strip in half lengthwise, wrong sides together; press. Divide strip into fourths and mark with pins, using seams as two of the marks.

Continued

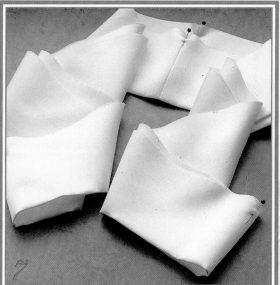

8 Stitch row of gathering stitches scant ½" (1.3 cm) from raw edges of strip; stitch second row ¼" (6 mm) closer to edges. Pin edge of strip to edge of pillow top, matching quarter marks on strip to corners of pillow. Pull up gathering threads so ruffle fits pillow top; distribute fullness evenly, and pin. Stitch ruffle to pillow scant ½" (1.3 cm) from edges.

9 Cut 11" (28 cm) square for pillow back. Center ribbon handle over pillow back, right sides up; baste ends within side seam allowances. Pin pillow front to pillow back, right sides together. Stitch ½" (1.3 cm) seam; leave opening for turning and stuffing. Turn right side out. Insert pillow form or stuff firmly with polyester fiberfill. Stitch opening closed. Tie wedding rings into ribbon tie.

Making a Potpourri Pillow

YOU WILL NEED

- ½ YD. (0.5 M) SHEER FABRIC, SUCH AS TULLE OR ORGANDY
- 2½ YD. (2.3 M) RIBBON, ¼" TO ⅜" (6 MM TO 1 CM) WIDE
- SILK FLOWERS; SMALL PEARLS
- POTPOURRI

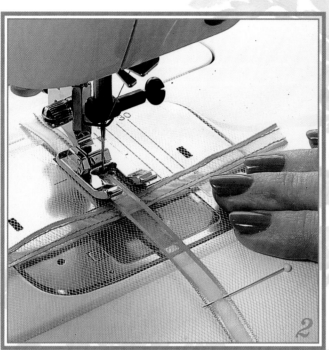

Cut two 13" (33 cm) squares of sheer fabric. Draw lines 2½" (6.5 cm) from each edge of each square, for flange.

1

Cut four 13" (33 cm) lengths of ribbon; pin to pillow top with inner edges along marked lines. Edgestitch both sides of each ribbon.

2

Remove silk flowers from stems. Arrange flowers randomly, right side up, on wrong side of pillow back, in flange area, avoiding seam allowances. Hand-stitch in place; stitch pearls in flower centers, if desired.

3

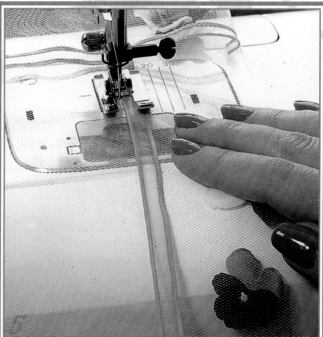

4 Pin pillow top and bottom, right sides together; stitch ½" (1.3 cm) seam; leave 5" (12.5 cm) opening in center of one side. Trim seams to ¼" (6 mm). Turn right side out, and press.

5 Pin top and bottom layers together along ribbons. Stitch around square just inside ribbons, to create flange; leave 5" (12.5 cm) opening parallel to outer opening.

6 Cut two 8" (20.5 cm) squares of sheer fabric; align edges, and stitch together in ¼" (6 mm) seam, leaving small opening. Turn right side out; fill with potpourri, and stitch opening closed.

7 Insert potpourri bag into center square of pillow. Pin inner opening closed; topstitch. Slipstitch outer opening closed.

8 Cut 8½" (21.8 cm) ribbon for handle; turn under ends ¼" (6 mm). Center ribbon over pillow back, and hand-stitch ends to fabric.

Cut 24" (61 cm) ribbon for ring tie; hand-stitch ribbon center to corner of square, where ribbons cross. Tie wedding rings into ribbon tie.

9

YOU WILL NEED

- 1/3 YD. (0.32 M) FABRIC
- POLYESTER FIBERFILL
- 1 1/4 YD. (1.15 M) GATHERED LACE, 4 1/2" (11.5 CM) WIDE
- SILK RIBBONS AND SEED BEADS FOR EMBROIDERY, AS INDICATED IN PATTERN
- 11" (28 CM) SATIN RIBBON, 1/2" (1.3 CM) WIDE, FOR HANDLE
- CHENILLE NEEDLE, SIZE 20 OR 22
- BEADING THREAD; BEADING NEEDLE
- LIQUID FRAY PREVENTER

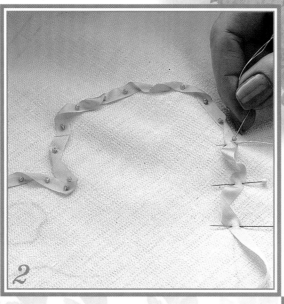

1 Trace heart pattern (opposite); add 3/8" (1 cm) seam allowance, and cut out. Trace pattern onto fabric twice, for front and back of pillow. Transfer embroidery design to front; do not cut out.

2 Thread beading needle with double strand of beading thread; knot end. Place end of 7 mm ribbon at beginning of heart outline (arrow); pull needle up from underside through ribbon. Thread seed bead onto needle, and insert needle back down through ribbon, near entry point. Continue stitching ribbon outline, twisting ribbon occasionally and securing to fabric with seed beads.

3 Embroider stitches of design, as on pages 72 to 75. Embroider roses first, then buds and leaves; fill in with vines.

4 Cut 18" (46 cm) length of 7 mm ribbon for ring tie. Stitch center of ribbon to center of heart. Cut out pillow front and back.

5 Fold under one short end of gathered lace ¼" (6 mm). Pin lace to pillow top edge, right sides together, starting at center top. Fold under excess lace at other end; trim to ¼" (6 mm). Baste lace to heart ¼" (6 mm) from edges. Hand-stitch ends together.

6 Center ribbon handle over pillow back, right sides up; baste ends within side seam allowances. Pin pillow front to pillow back, right sides together. Stitch ⅜" (1 cm) seam; leave opening for turning and stuffing. Stitch again over seam at center top; clip seam allowance to stitching. Apply liquid fray preventer to point of clip.

7 Turn pillow right side out, and stuff firmly with fiberfill. Stitch opening closed. Tie wedding rings into ribbon tie.

Fold

Start

Spiderweb rose

Stem stitch

Loop stitch

Japanese ribbon stitch

- 2 YD. (1.85 M) PINK SILK RIBBON, 7 MM WIDE
- 3 YD. (2.75 M) DARK PURPLE SILK RIBBON, 4 MM WIDE
- 3 YD. (2.75 M) LIGHT PURPLE SILK RIBBON, 4 MM WIDE
- 3 YD. (2.75 M) GREEN SILK RIBBON, 4 MM WIDE
- 55 PINK SEED BEADS
- 35 PURPLE SEED BEADS

BRIDAL & ATTENDANT
Bouquets

*A lovely bouquet that is easy
to assemble is the hand-tied European bouquet.*

A hand-tied European bouquet has the fresh-from-the-garden, just-picked look. Tie the stems with a ribbon or raffia bow for simplicity, or wrap the stems with ribbon to create an elegant, sleek line. Both the bride's and the attendants' bouquets can be made in this style; just vary the look by varying the kind, color, and amount of flowers. Bouquets can also be made using artificial or dried flowers.

Order fresh flowers ahead of time from a florist; these will come specially treated to last. Cut the stems to 12" to 15" (30.5 to 38 cm) in length; cut them at an angle, using a sharp knife, not a scissors. Put the stems into a vase of fresh, tepid water mixed with flower preservative. Rose stems must be placed into water within 10 seconds of cutting.

After making the bouquet, keep the stems in water mixed with preservative, and wrap them just before the ceremony, if a ribbon wrap is desired.

FRESH FLOWER SUGGESTIONS

TYPE	OPTIONS
FLOWERS	MINIATURE OR STANDARD ROSES OR CARNATIONS, LILIES, CALLA LILIES, LILY OF THE VALLEY, DENDROBIUM OR CYMBIDIUM ORCHIDS, STEPHANOTIS, HYDRANGEAS, IRISES, FREESIA, SMALLER VARIETIES OF CHRYSANTHEMUMS, RANUNCULUS
GREENS	PLUMOSA FERN, GALAX LEAVES, LEATHERLEAF FERN, CEDAR, SEEDED EUCALYPTUS
FILLERS	BABY'S BREATH, LIMONIUM, CASPIA, STATICE, GOLDEN ASTER, WAX FLOWER

YOU WILL NEED

- FLOWERS
- GREENS
- FILLER FLOWERS
- RIBBON OR RAFFIA
- GREEN FLORAL TAPE OR GREEN WATERPROOF TAPE
- 24-GAUGE GREEN PADDLE WIRE
- KNIFE
- VASE OF FRESH, TEPID WATER MIXED WITH PRESERVATIVE

1 Cut ribbon or raffia to desired length, if not using a stem wrap. If using roses, break off thorns with finger or knife.

2 Hold group of flowers that will form center of bouquet in your secondary hand. Wrap paddle wire around stems several times, 3" to 4" (7.5 to 10 cm) below flower heads; wrap snugly, but avoid cutting stems.

3 Add individual flowers, greens, and fillers one at a time; lay new stem across other stems at slight angle where stems are held with secondary hand. Evenly distribute flowers around cluster, turning bouquet with each addition. Start each row slightly lower than previous row. Wrap stems occasionally with paddle wire to secure.

4 Add galax or plumosa leaves all around bouquet when desired shape is reached. Tape all stems together three or four times with floral tape where hand is holding bouquet. If a ribbon wrap for stems is desired, omit step 5.

5 | Tie ribbon or raffia over area wrapped with floral tape, and tie into a bow.

6 | Cut flower stems 4" to 6" (10 to 15 cm) below tape, and place in vase of fresh, tepid water with preservative. Remove from vase and dry with towel just before ceremony. Apply plain ribbon wrap (below), ballet wrap (page 106), or laced wrap (page 107), if desired.

Applying a Plain Ribbon Wrap

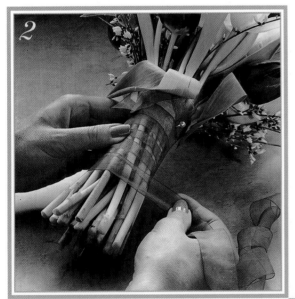

1 | Cut 3 to 5 yd. (2.75 to 4.6 m) of tulle ribbon, 5" (12.5 cm) wide, or organza ribbon, 1½" to 2¾" (3.8 to 7 cm) wide, or any width florist satin ribbon; length depends on width of ribbon and size of bow desired.

2 | Place one end of ribbon over area wrapped with floral tape, and push a 1½" (3.8 cm) pearl-headed pin through ribbon and stems. Wrap ribbon around stems in a spiral, angling slightly downward and overlapping wraps by ½" (1.3 cm).

3 | Insert pearl-headed pin up into bottom of stems through ribbon; wrap ribbon back up stems in a spiral pattern.

4 | Knot ends of ribbon; cut off excess, and tuck under knotted area. Wrap remaining ribbon around knotted area; tie into bow.

Ceremony Accents

105

1 Cut 3 to 5 yd. (2.75 to 4.6 m) of florist satin ribbon, ⅝" (1.5 cm) wide; length depends on size of bow desired.

2 Place one end of ribbon over area wrapped with floral tape, and push a 1½" (3.8 cm) pearl-headed pin through ribbon and stems; leave tail for tying. Wrap ribbon around stems in a spiral, angling downward; leave 1" (2.5 cm) space between wraps.

3 Insert a 1½" (3.8 cm) pearl-headed pin through ribbon and up into stems at bottom, to anchor. Wrap ribbon back up stems, crossing downward wraps at aligned points. Stems will show between wraps.

4 Knot ends of ribbon; cut off excess. Wrap remaining ribbon around knotted area, and tie into a bow.

Cut 3 to 4 yd. (2.75 to 3.7 m) of wide sheer ribbon; length depends on size of bow desired. Anchor ribbon end over taped area, inserting 1½" (3.8 cm) pearl-headed pin upward into stems; leave tail for tying.

1

Insert vertical row of pearl-headed pins upward into stems, below first pin; space pins 1" (2.5 cm) apart. Cut off pin points, using wire cutter if they are too long.

2

Wrap ribbon around back of stems; bring to front, and loop around second pearl head. Wrap back around stems in opposite direction, and loop around third pearl head. Continue lacing ribbon in this manner to bottom pearl head.

3

Loop ribbon around bottom pearl head; wrap around stems and loop around same pearl head from opposite direction. Lace ribbon back up stems and loop around heads, as in step 3, wrapping from the opposite side.

4

Knot ribbon ends at top of stems; anchor with pin. Wrap remaining ribbon around knotted area, and tie into a bow.

5

Corsages & *Boutonnieres*

Corsages and boutonnieres honor those who wear them and tie in with the look of the wedding.

Pretty corsages and festive boutonnieres can be made inexpensively from flowers and greens purchased from a florist. Artificial flowers and greens, available from craft stores, can also be used.

Order fresh flowers ahead of time from a florist; these will come specially treated to last. Cut off ½" to 1" (1.3 to 2.5 cm) of the stems at an angle, using a sharp knife, not a scissors. Put the stems into a vase of fresh, tepid water mixed with flower preservative. Rose stems must be placed into water within 10 seconds of cutting.

In preparation for making corsages and boutonnieres, first wire and wrap the stems. Select the appropriate method, depending on whether the flower has a deep or shallow calyx under the flower head. Most artificial flowers and greens don't need to be wired. When you are finished, mist fresh-flower corsages and boutonnieres, and store them in the refrigerator in a sealed plastic bag. Label each bag with the wearer's name.

Attach the corsages on the wearer's left side using a 2" (5 cm) corsage pin. Pin it to the clothing, in the natural curvature of the body, high in the shoulder area. Insert the pin through the top third of the corsage so it will not tip over, and pin through to a shoulder pad or undergarment strap for support, if possible.

Attach a boutonniere using a 1½" (3.8 cm) black-headed boutonniere pin. Insert the pin from the underside of the widest part of the lapel on the wearer's left side.

Tip

MAKE AN EXTRA BOUTONNIERE AND CORSAGE FOR SOMEONE YOU MAY HAVE FORGOTTEN OR FOR AN UNEXPECTED SPECIAL GUEST WHO MAY ARRIVE.

Fresh Flower Suggestions

Type	Options
FLOWERS	MINIATURE OR STANDARD ROSES OR CARNATIONS, ALSTROMERIA, DENDROBIUM ORCHIDS, POMPOM OR DAISY CHRYSANTHEMUMS
GREENS	PLUMOSA OR LEATHERLEAF FERN, ITALIAN RUSCUS, IVY
FILLERS	BABY'S BREATH, LIMONIUM, CASPIA, STATICE, GOLDEN ASTER, WAX FLOWER

Wiring a Flower with a Deep Calyx

1 | Cut off flower stem approximately 1" (2.5 cm) below flower head.

2 | Cut a 24-gauge floral stem wire in half. Pierce flower through side of calyx, just below flower head, with wire. Push wire halfway through calyx, and bend both ends of wire down along stem.

3 | Insert remaining wire through calyx at a right angle to first wire, if flower bends over or is wobbly when held upright. This occurs with heavier flowers, such as a standard, full-size rose.

4 | Place end of ½" (1.3 cm) wide floral tape on back side of flower calyx as close to flower head as possible; hold in place with index finger. Wrap tape once around stem, gently stretching tape; press tape onto itself. Warmth of fingers softens paraffin in tape, causing it to stick.

Twist flower, so tape spirals around stem; pull tape gently, stretching and warming it between thumb and index finger. Work tape down stem to bottom of wire, wrapping at a slightly downward angle. Break off tape and smooth over wire end.

5

Wiring a Flower with a Shallow Calyx

Follow step 1, opposite. Cut a 24-gauge floral stem wire in half. Bend one end into a small hook.

1

Pierce center top of flower with straight end of wire. Gently push wire down through flower and stem until hook disappears inside flower. Tape flower as in steps 4 and 5, opposite and above.

2

Making a Boutonniere

YOU WILL NEED

- FLOWERS
- GREENS
- 24-GAUGE FLORAL STEM WIRE

- FLORAL TAPE, ½" (1.3 CM) WIDE
- WIRE CUTTER
- BOUTONNIERE PIN

1 Tape and wire flowers as on pages 110 and 111. Cut a 24-gauge floral stem wire in half. Cut greens stem several inches (centimeters) longer than the desired finished size of the boutonniere.

2 Bend one wire in half; slip over greens stem at a point ⅔ of the way up from bottom of stem. Wrap doubled-over wire together with greens stem, using floral tape, as on pages 110 and 111, steps 4 and 5.

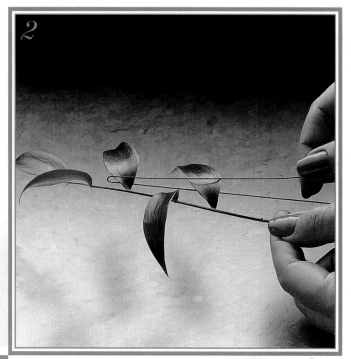

3 Lay flower on top of greens stem, leaving about 1" (2.5 cm) of greens showing above flower. Wrap tops of stems together twice with floral tape. Place stems of smaller pieces of greens to sides and bottom of flower, if more fullness is desired.

4 Wrap all stems together as on page 111, step 5. Cut stems about 1½" (3.8 cm) below bottom of flower head, using wire cutter. Smooth tape over end of wire.

YOU WILL NEED

- FLOWERS
- GREENS
- FILLER FLOWERS, IF DESIRED
- 24-GAUGE FLORAL STEM WIRE
- WIRE CUTTER
- CORSAGE PIN

1 Wire and tape flowers, as on pages 110 and 111; wire and tape greens backing piece as in step 2, opposite.

2 Lay smallest flower on top of greens, leaving about 1" (2.5 cm) of greens showing above flower. Secure top of flower stem and greens stem together with floral tape, as on page 110, step 4, wrapping tape twice.

3 Place next largest flower to the right of and slightly below top flower. Wrap all stems together twice with floral tape. Place filler flower or small greens next to flower, if desired; secure with floral tape.

4 Repeat step 3 for third flower, placing flower slightly lower and left of top flower.

5 Repeat steps 3 and 4 until desired length of corsage is reached; add a ribbon bow, if desired. An uneven number of flowers usually works best for balance.

6 Wrap all stems together as on page 111, step 5. Cut stems about 1½" (3.8 cm) below bottom of lowest flower head, using wire cutter. Smooth tape over end of wire.

PEW

Accents

Ribbons or wreaths hung from pews at the church, synagogue, or other ceremony location lend beauty and elegance to the walk down the aisle.

And after the ceremony, transport these same adornments to the reception site; use wreaths for centerpieces, and attach bows to table skirts or use them as wall decorations.

Make pew decorations as simple or as elaborate as you wish. Place a decoration on every pew, every other pew, or every third pew. Adorn them with fresh, artificial, or dried flowers and greens.

Attach pew accents with rubber bands, rings made from pipe cleaners, or pew clips. Check with the facility to see how the tops of the pews are constructed; a ledge, pew cap, or other surface is needed from which to hang accents. Some facilities allow the use of tape, but get approval beforehand, as tape can mar surfaces.

Use bow accents also to adorn candelabras; run a pipe cleaner through the back loop of the bow and wrap it around the candelabra.

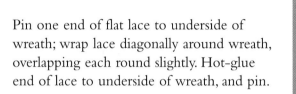

Making a Pew Wreath

YOU WILL NEED

- 10" (25.5 CM) STYROFOAM® WREATH
- 3 YD. (2.75 M) FLAT LACE, 2" (5 CM) WIDE
- 1 YD. (0.95 M) DOUBLE RUFFLE LACE, 3" (7.5 CM) WIDE
- SILK IVY
- 3 TO 5 SILK FLOWERS, 2" TO 4" (5 TO 10 CM) WIDE

- BABY'S BREATH
- 1¼ YD. (1.15 M) WIRED RIBBON, 3" (7.5 CM) WIDE
- 26-GAUGE CRAFT WIRE
- HOT GLUE GUN OR CRAFT GLUE
- PEW CLIP, PIPE CLEANER, RIBBON, OR RUBBER BAND, FOR HANGING

1 Pin one end of flat lace to underside of wreath; wrap lace diagonally around wreath, overlapping each round slightly. Hot-glue end of lace to underside of wreath, and pin.

2 Hot-glue binding of double ruffle lace to outer edge of underside of wreath, easing lace generously around wreath. Overlap ends about 1½" (3.8 cm); glue.

3 Cut 27" (68.5 cm) of wired ribbon for streamers. Shape remaining wired ribbon into bow; pinch center and secure with craft wire. Fold streamer in half over bow; secure to bow with hot glue. Hot-glue bow to wreath, and push a pin through bow into wreath. Cut ends of streamers at angles.

4 Form 6" (15 cm) sprig of ivy into a circle and hot-glue to center of bow. Hot-glue one large flower inside ivy circle. Hot-glue other flowers around bow.

5 Hot-glue 10" (25.5 cm) sprigs of ivy to each side of wreath, starting under bow and following curve of wreath. Hot-glue baby's breath sprigs among ivy leaves. Hot-glue hanger to top back of wreath.

Making a Tulle Bow

YOU WILL NEED

- 1 YD. (0.95 M) ILLUSION, 72" (183 CM) WIDE
- LARGE RUBBER BAND, PIPE CLEANER, OR PEW CLIP, FOR HANGING
- 6 YD. (5.5 M) RIBBON, ¼" (6 MM) WIDE
- WIRED RIBBON, ⅝" TO 2¼" (1.5 TO 6 CM) WIDE, FOR RIBBON ROSES
- HOT GLUE

1 Open up illusion and tie into bow, using width of fabric as length of bow. Pouf out bow.

2 Pull rubber band through loop in back of bow, for hanger.

3 Cut six 1-yd. (0.95 m) pieces of ¼" (6 mm) ribbon; knot together at center. Hot-glue to center of bow. Knot ribbon ends.

4 Make one or more ribbon roses (page 118), using ⅝" to 2¼" (1.5 to 6 cm) wide ribbon, depending on size desired; hot-glue to center of illusion bow.

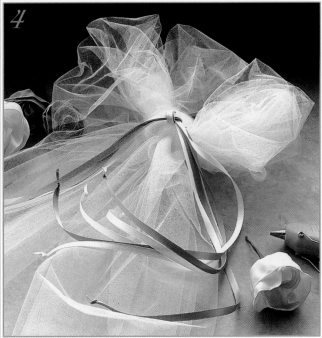

Making Ribbon Roses

YOU WILL NEED
- WIRED RIBBON IN DESIRED WIDTH
- MEDIUM-GAUGE STEM WIRE
- ARTIFICIAL ROSE LEAVES, IF DESIRED
- FLORAL TAPE

1 Bend a 1" (2.5 cm) loop in end of stem wire; twist to secure. Cut desired length of wired ribbon; cut 16" (40.5 cm) of ⅝" (1.5 cm) ribbon; cut 32" (81.5 cm) of 1½" (3.8 cm) ribbon; cut 1½ yd. (1.4 m) of 2¼" (6 cm) ribbon.

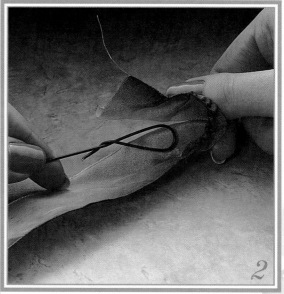

2 Pull out about 2" (5 cm) of wire on one edge of one end of ribbon. Fold that ribbon end over loop; wrap pulled wire around ribbon at bottom of loop, forming rose center.

3 Gather up one edge of remaining length of ribbon tightly by sliding ribbon along ribbon wire toward the rose center.

4 Wrap gathered edge around base of rose, wrapping each layer slightly higher than previous layer.

5 Fold the ribbon end down and catch under last layer. Wrap ribbon wire tightly around base several times to secure. Cut off excess ribbon wire. For flower without stem, cut off stem wire and omit step 7.

6 Wrap floral tape end around base of rose, stretching tape slightly for best adhesion. Wrap entire base of rose, concealing wire.

7 Continue wrapping floral tape onto stem wire. Place artificial rose leaf next to stem wire; wrap leaf stem and wire together with floral tape. Continue wrapping until entire stem wire is covered with floral tape.

Variations

SWAGS

Create swags down center aisle by draping tulle yardage or ribbons between pew accents. Usher guests into pews from side aisle before the ceremony. After the ceremony, remove the draping before the guests are released down the center aisle.

RIBBON ACCENTS

Combine two wide ribbons and tie them into large bows. Hot-glue flowers or greens into centers of bows.

Tip

HAVE ONE OR SEVERAL PEOPLE ASSIGNED TO TRANSPORT PEW ACCENTS TO THE RECEPTION SITE, AND ALLOW ENOUGH TIME FOR THEM TO SET UP ITEMS BEFORE GUESTS ARRIVE.

A WEDDING

Arbor

A decorated arbor at the ceremony entrance creates an enchanting ambience.

It welcomes your guests, focuses attention on a special area, and serves as a lovely backdrop for photographs.

Purchase a simple multipiece arch framework at a garden center or from the bridal department of a fabric store. Decorate it in sections with silk, fresh, or dried flowers and greens, ribbons, or tulle. The arbor can then be transported and assembled in its intended location on the day of the wedding. Wrap the arbor with tiny twinkling lights for an evening wedding. For stability, anchor the ends in containers of cement. Or, for an outdoor wedding, anchor them in the ground.

When using fresh flowers, select large, showy blossoms; cut the stems to 3" (7.5 cm), and put them in water-filled tubes, available from florist or craft stores. Wire fresh or artificial flowers and greens onto the arbor; secure dried flowers with hot glue.

In addition, trellises and archways can be rented from party rental companies, florists, or places that rent props for special events. Decorate these with flowers, greens, lights, and tulle, as desired, but avoid using glue on rented arbors. If using lights on white lattice, choose strings with white cord.

Decorating an Arbor

YOU WILL NEED

- MULTIPIECE ARCH FRAMEWORK
- 2 TROUGHS, SUCH AS PLANTER BOX INSERTS, SLIGHTLY LONGER THAN ARCH BASE
- GARDEN TROWEL OR LONG-HANDLED COOKING SPOON
- QUICK-DRYING CEMENT
- FABRIC FOR COVERING OUTSIDE OF CONTAINER
- THIN BATTING
- SPANISH MOSS, FOR COVERING TOP OF CEMENT
- EMBELLISHMENTS, SUCH AS SILK, FRESH, OR DRIED FLOWERS, RIBBONS, OR TULLE
- 24-GAUGE WIRE
- HOT GLUE GUN

Assemble arch framework to desired height. Determine sections and points where arch can be easily separated and reassembled.

1

Plug any holes in troughs. Mix enough cement in each trough to come within 2" (5 cm) of rim, following manufacturer's directions.

2

Continued

3 Allow cement to set only slightly. Insert arch base into cement, centering it in trough. Hold or prop arch base in position until cement is set completely. Repeat for other base and trough.

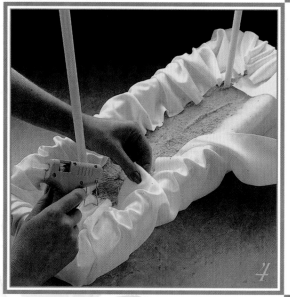

Cut fabric rectangle one-and-one-half times the outer trough measurements, measuring up over sides to cement. Stitch gathering threads lengthwise in center of rectangle, about one-and-one-half times the trough length. Pull up threads, gathering section evenly to length of trough; slip fabric under trough, centering gathers. Wrap trough with batting. Pleat fabric loosely, and wrap up over sides; hot-glue to cement. Repeat for other trough. 4

5 Cover cement and fabric edges with Spanish moss. Secure silk, fresh, or dried flowers to arbor, using wire or hot glue; cluster several flowers and greens at center top, creating focal point. Embellish with ribbons or tulle.

Historic Fact

IN PRIMITIVE TIMES, THE WEDDING CELEBRATION INCLUDED THE ENTIRE TOWN, TRIBE, OR VILLAGE AND LASTED FOR DAYS UNTIL EVERYONE COLLAPSED FROM EXHAUSTION.

Variations
ON THE THEME

SPARKLING TWIG ARBOR
Anchor several birch or willow branches in buckets of cement. Wrap the buckets with batting, and swath them with tulle. Coil twinkle lights and tulle around the branches.

FLOWER-ADORNED LATTICE ARCH
Select large and showy flowers, such as carnations, lilies, roses, hydrangeas, chrysanthemums, statice, and asters. Cut flower stem to 3" (7.5 cm) long, and place in tubes filled with fresh water, if using fresh flowers. Wire onto lattice in a random pattern, using 26-gauge wire. Select hardy fresh greens, such as tree branches, salal, sprenghri or plumosa fern, or artificial ivy or ferns; wire to lattice.

STAGING A RECEPTION

*Formal or casual, indoors or out,
the reception honors the new couple as
they welcome their guests. Tasteful
decorations and thoughtful details
enhance the wedding celebration.*

FRESH FLORAL
Table Wreaths

When paired together in a table wreath, flowers and candles transform the mood of a room.

Fresh floral table wreaths dress up the head table, guest tables, or buffet. Wreaths are easily assembled by covering a foam wreath form with greens, then inserting floral stems into the foam. A group of pillar candles, or one candle encased in a hurricane lamp, light up the center.

Tip

PRIOR TO THE WEDDING, DECIDE WHO WILL TAKE HOME THE CENTERPIECES TO ENJOY AFTER THE RECEPTION.

YOU WILL NEED

- IVY
- HONEYSUCKLE VINES
- ROSES
- FREESIA
- STATICE
- SMILAX GARLAND
- LEATHERLEAF FERN
- SHEET MOSS
- FOAM WREATH FORM FOR FRESH FLOWERS; FLORAL PINS
- GROUPING OF PILLAR CANDLES TO FIT WITHIN CENTER OF WREATH FORM

1. Soak foam wreath form in water until saturated; dampen the sheet moss. Cover wreath form with sheet moss; secure with floral pins.

2. Drape ivy stems over wreath; secure with floral pins. Insert stems of leatherleaf fern into wreath; cut small openings in moss with a knife, if necessary, so stems can be inserted easily.

3. Cut honeysuckle vine into desired lengths. Insert both ends into foam, maintaining curve of vine and spacing vines randomly.

4. Cut stems of roses about 2" (5 cm) long, cutting them diagonally under water with sharp knife. Insert stems into floral foam, spacing them evenly.

5. Cut stems of freesia about 2" (5 cm) long, cutting them diagonally with sharp knife. Insert the stems into floral foam, spacing them evenly. Repeat for statice, filling in any bare areas.

6. Mist wreath with water; place on layers of newspaper for several hours, to soak up excess water. Or display the wreath on a platter. Place a grouping of pillar candles in center of wreath.

Staging a Reception

Variations

ON THE THEME

SILK FLOWER WREATH ▶

Cover a floral Styrofoam® wreath form with silk flowers and greens, varying the shapes and textures of the elements.

HOLIDAY THEME

Make a fresh table wreath, using holly and ivy. Embellish with berries.

DRIED FLOWER WREATH

Decorate a moss-covered wreath with clusters of dried roses, using hot glue; add smaller elements, and fill in with statice or baby's breath. Accent with feathery doves.

MIRROR TILE
Centerpieces

Simple, but enchanting, centerpieces can be created using mirror tiles as a base.

A tulle wreath encircling a candle makes a pretty centerpiece over a mirror tile, and can double as a pew accent during the wedding ceremony.

Flowers, greens, ribbons, and tulle, lovely in centerpieces, have twice the effect when reflected in a mirror tile base. Candles help set the mood and add a romantic warm glow. Confetti sprinkled about gives the table a festive look; potpourri offers a delightful scent. Flowers may be fresh, artificial, dried, or made from ribbon, as on page 118.

Reception sites or catering companies often rent or loan square, oval, or round mirrors. Home improvement stores also carry 12" (30.5 cm) square mirror tiles.

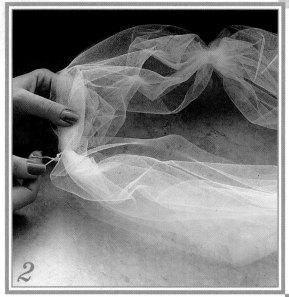

YOU WILL NEED

- MIRROR TILE
- TULLE RECTANGLE, 48" × 24" (122 × 61 CM)
- 9 ARTIFICIAL, DRIED, OR FRESH FLOWER HEADS, 1" (2.5 CM) WIDE
- 1⅓ YD. (1.27 M) PEARL STRING, 4 MM WIDE
- 1⅓ YD. (1.27 M) SATIN RIBBON, ⅛" (3 MM) WIDE
- WHITE COVERED WIRE
- HOT GLUE GUN OR CRAFT GLUE
- CANDLEHOLDER AND CANDLE

1 Cut tulle into one 36" × 24" (91.5 × 61 cm) rectangle and three 3" × 24" (7.5 × 61 cm) strips for each wreath.

2 Overlap short ends of large rectangle slightly, and wrap tightly together with wire. Wrap wire tightly around tulle at 12" (30.5 cm) intervals. Pouf out each section.

3 Trim flower stems to ½" (1.3 cm). Place three flower heads in center of narrow tulle strip; glue in place. Gather tulle with fingers to form a rosette around flowers; wrap wire tightly around base of rosette. Wire or glue flower rosette to wreath over wire-wrapped area. Repeat for other two flower rosettes.

4 Glue one end of pearl string under one rosette; wrap pearl string around wreath, wrapping twice between each rosette. Glue end of pearl string under first rosette. Repeat with satin ribbon.

5 Place tulle cloud on mirror tile; put desired candleholder and candle in center of cloud.

Tip

IF USING FRESH FLOWERS, MAKE THE MOST OF YOUR FLORAL BUDGET BY CHOOSING BLOOMS THAT ARE IN SEASON AND LOCALLY GROWN.

Staging a Reception

131

Votive Candleholders with Flowers and Greens

YOU WILL NEED

- MIRROR TILE
- RIBBON
- FRESH OR ARTIFICIAL GREENS, SUCH AS LEATHER LEAF, PLUMOSA, SPRENGHRI FERN, IVY, OR ITALIAN RUSCUS
- FRESH FLOWERS, SUCH AS MINIATURE ROSES, CARNATIONS, IRISES, LILIES, DAISY AND CUSHION CHRYSANTHEMUMS, AND ASTERS; OR ARTIFICIAL OR DRIED FLOWERS AS DESIRED
- FRESH, ARTIFICIAL, OR DRIED FILLER FLOWERS, SUCH AS BABY'S BREATH, LIMONIUM, AND CASPIA
- TWO VOTIVE CANDLEHOLDERS WITH CANDLES
- CONFETTI OR POTPOURRI, IF DESIRED

Place greens diagonally across mirror in a slight S-shape. Twirl lengths of ribbon and lay over greens. Add flowers and fillers, following line of greens.

1

Place a votive candleholder on each side of diagonal of greens. Scatter confetti or potpourri over mirror tile, if desired.

2

Variations

ON THE THEME

SIMPLE ELEGANCE

Tie a ribbon bow to the long stems of two or three flowers, such as calla lillies or roses. Place diagonally on the mirror tile.

HURRICANE LAMP

Place candle and hurricane lamp in center of mirror tile. Lay greens around base of hurricane lamp. Twirl lengths of ribbon through greens. Scatter individual blooms or clusters of small flowers over greens.

CARD *Holders*

Decorate a special container to hold cards from your guests.

Place it on the gift table at the reception as both an item of convenience and an element of the decor. Decorate the box in a style that fits the theme of the wedding. Glue fabric and trims directly to the cardboard, as for the hat-box-style holder, below. Or, follow the directions for making a padded card box.

Making a Padded Card Box

YOU WILL NEED

- BOX WITH FOLD-DOWN FLAPS ON TOP AND BOTTOM, APPROXIMATELY 12" × 16" × 10" (30.5 × 40.5 × 25.5 CM)
- CLEAR MAILING TAPE
- UTILITY KNIFE

- 1¼ YD. (1.15 M) FABRIC, 60" (152.5 CM) WIDE
- 1½ YD. (1.4 M) POLYFLEECE
- 3 YD. (2.75 M) NARROW PEARL-EDGED SATIN RIBBON
- 3 YD. (2.75 M) SHEER RIBBON,

- 1½" (3.8 CM) WIDE
- SILK FLOWERS AND LEAVES
- ASSORTED PEARL SPRAYS; WIRED PEARL HEARTS
- HOT GLUE GUN; CRAFT GLUE
- LIQUID FRAY PREVENTER

1 Tape box closed. Cut opening in center top of box 6" (15 cm) long and ¾" (2 cm) wide, using utility knife.

2 Cut two pieces of polyfleece to same size as box ends. Cut strip of polyfleece to wrap vertically around box, with width equal to box length.

3 Glue smaller pieces of polyfleece to box ends, using craft glue. Wrap larger piece of polyfleece around rest of box, butting edges over opening; glue to box. Cut slits in polyfleece over ends of opening, and roll flaps to inside of box; glue in place.

4 Wrap fabric around box, as if wrapping gift; glue in place.

Continued

5 Mark cutting line over opening as shown. Apply liquid fray preventer over marked line; allow to dry. Cut slit; roll fabric to inside, and glue.

6 Drape narrow pearl ribbon over box top and down sides, as desired. Glue ribbon to box every 2" to 3" (5 to 7.5 cm), twisting and looping ribbon occasionally.

7 Cut wide sheer ribbon into two pieces, and tie into bows. Hot-glue bows to opposite corners of box top; drape and hot-glue tails around box sides every 3" to 4" (7.5 to 10 cm), twisting and looping ribbon.

8 Glue pearl sprays under each bow. Arrange silk flower clusters over each bow; hot-glue. Arrange smaller flower clusters and pearl sprays at each end of opening; hot-glue in place.

Tip

KEEP A CARD FILE OF THE NAMES AND ADDRESSES OF THE GUESTS. THE FILE WILL COME IN HANDY WHEN WRITING INVITATIONS AND THANK-YOU CARDS, IF ON EACH CARD YOU NOTE THE GIFT THAT WAS GIVEN.

Variations

ON THE THEME

BIRDCAGE CARDHOLDER

Secure sheet moss around the base of a fancy birdcage, using hot glue. Arrange dried flowers, pods, and berries over the moss, for a natural, woodsy style. Cluster more dried flowers at the top of the cage, along with a large sheer bow. Trail ribbon tails down the sides of the cage.

MAILBOX

Decorate a white mailbox with pine branches, ribbons, and papier mâché birds.

Julia and Mike

CHAMPAGNE
Bottle Cover

A champagne bottle cover dresses up the table at the reception or rehearsal dinner. Set beside an array of glasses, candles, or a flower centerpiece, it lends a touch of elegance.

Select a rich fabric such as jacquard, shantung, or satin and a coordinating lining fabric. Interline the cover with polyfleece for additional body and insulation. To tie off the bottle neck in style, select a chair tie in the appropriate color. Available in the home decorating department of fabric stores, this 27" (68.5 cm) length of decorative cording has a tassel at each end.

Making a Champagne Bottle Cover

YOU WILL NEED

- ½ YD. (0.5 M) OUTER FABRIC
- ½ YD. (0.5 M) LINING FABRIC
- ½ YD. (0.5 M) POLYFLEECE
- CHAIR TIE

1 | Cut a rectangle 18" × 16" (46 × 40.5 cm) of fabric, polyfleece, and lining. Baste polyfleece to wrong side of fabric.

2 | Fold fabric in half, right sides together, aligning longer edges; pin. Stitch ¼" (6 mm) seam down back and across bottom. Repeat for lining, leaving 4" (10 cm) opening on side, for turning.

3 | Fold cover at bottom so seam is centered as shown; pin. Mark a line 2" (5 cm) in from point, perpendicular to seam. Repeat for opposite point.

Continued

Historic Fact

ETIQUETTE SAYS THAT, EXCEPT FOR THE CHAMPAGNE TOAST THAT ACCOMPANIES CAKE CUTTING, THE BRIDE AND GROOM SHOULD NOT SIP FROM THEIR GLASSES WHEN THEY ARE TOASTED. CLINKING GLASSES TOGETHER AFTER A TOAST WAS ORIGINALLY INTENDED TO PRODUCE A BELL-LIKE SOUND TO WARD OFF EVIL SPIRITS.

Making a Champagne Bottle Cover
(continued)

4 Stitch along marked lines; trim off points ¼"(6 mm) from stitching.

5 Repeat steps 3 and 4 for lining. Turn outer bag right side out. Place outer bag inside lining, right sides together, aligning upper edges; pin. Stitch ¼" (6 mm) from edges. Turn right side out through opening in lining. Slipstitch opening closed.

Tuck lining inside cover. Press upper edge. Topstitch ¼" (6 mm) from upper edge. **6**

Tack center of chair tie over center back seam of cover, 3" (7.5 cm) from top. Insert the bottle, and tie cord snugly around bottle neck. **7**

DECORATIVE BUTTON ACCENT
Stitch large, decorative shank button to center front of cover, 3" (7.5 cm) from top. Cross cords under button, and tie.

SILK FLOWER SPRAY
Attach several strands of ⅛" (3 mm) ribbon, 1 yd. (0.95 m) long, instead of chair tie. Tack ½" (1.3 cm) ring to back of silk flower spray; tack ring to center front of cover, 3" (7.5 cm) from top. Thread ribbons through ring, and tie together into a bow, behind flowers.

CAKE *Tops*

A floral arrangement for the top of the cake is an eye-catching adornment.

Flowers look beautiful on top of the wedding cake. Cake tops can be decorated with fresh or artificial flowers placed directly on the icing or arranged first in a small, clean plastic container, such as the cover of an aerosol can, that is gently placed on the cake. To anchor fresh flowers in their container, use fresh floral foam; for artificial flowers, use Styrofoam®.

If the layers of the cake are separated with spacers, or multiple cakes will be grouped for display, each can be decorated with flowers and greens; adjust the amount of decoration with the size of each layer or cake.

Tip

FIND SOURCES FOR GOOD BAKERS BY ASKING YOUR PHOTOGRAPHER, FLORIST, OR RECEPTION SITE. BECAUSE THESE PROFESSIONALS ATTEND A LOT OF RECEPTIONS, THEY SEE AND HEAR ABOUT THE BEST AND THE WORST WEDDING CAKES.

Decorating a Cake with Flowers

YOU WILL NEED

- FLOWERS
- GREENS, SUCH AS IVY OR ITALIAN RUSCUS
- PLASTIC CONTAINER OR CUP
- FRESH FLORAL FOAM OR STYROFOAM® SLIGHTLY LARGER THAN CONTAINER

1 Cut fresh floral foam if using fresh flowers, or Styrofoam if using artificial flowers, to fit snugly into container and approximately ¾" (2 cm) above edge. Insert foam into container; add water to fresh floral foam.

2 Cover foam with greens; allow greens to hang over edge to cover container.

3 Select flower that will be the tallest in the arrangement; trim stem to desired size with a sharp knife, and insert flower into foam.

4 Trim stems of additional flowers to desired size, and insert flowers around tallest flower, making a somewhat rounded arrangement.

5 Gently place container onto top layer of cake after cake has been positioned and displayed properly on its table.

6 If cake has multiple layers with spacers in between, put greens on succeeding layers, and lay flowers on top of greens.

7 Lay greens and flowers around base of cake to balance display and to create a division between cake and tablecloth, thus adding dimension and importance to cake.

Variations

ON THE THEME

DELLA ROBBIA EFFECT

Cluster purchased marzipan fruits on the tops of individually displayed cakes. Select fruits of the same scale in a size large enough to be impressive, but not overpowering; use smaller clusters on smaller cakes. Arrange fresh greens around the base of the largest cake, interspersed with more marzipan fruit.

SLIPCOVERED
Chairs

*Dress up chairs at the head table
with softly draping fabric slipcovers.*

Quick and easy slipcovers transform simple chairs
into elegant seating for members of the wedding
party. Tied with wide ribbon or knotted in a
pouf, inexpensive fabric adds a formal touch to
the reception.

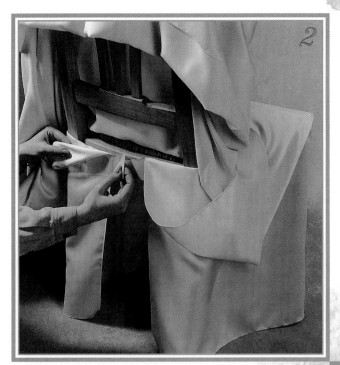

YOU WILL NEED

- FABRIC, SUCH AS INEXPENSIVE SATIN OR TAFFETA
- 3 YD. (2.75 M) WIRED RIBBON
- 1½ YD. (1.4 M) NARROW RIBBON OR STRING
- WIDE MASKING TAPE; SAFETY PINS

Cut fabric length equal to the continuous distance from floor up front of chair, over seat to back, and up and over back to floor plus 2" (5 cm). Stitch narrow hems in ends and sides, or serge, if necessary.

1

2 Drape fabric, centered, over chair, smoothing fabric to back of seat. Wrap lower portion around to chair back; tape as shown.

3 Wrap narrow ribbon or string around chair and fabric to back of seat; knot securely. Arrange folds; pin at center back. Wrap wired ribbon over narrow ribbon; knot securely, and tie into bow, leaving long tails. Or, grasp fabric at center back; tie into knot, and pouf out fabric as shown, opposite, top.

Tip

PLACE A SLIPCOVERED CHAIR IN THE WOMEN'S POWDER ROOM AS AN ELEGANT EXTRA TOUCH.

Staging a Reception

TABLE

Favors

Handcrafted favor bags and boxes are a delightful treat for guests.

Festive favor bags and boxes are fun to set out on tables at the reception; fill them with candy, sugared almonds, or petits fours. They can also be filled with rice, dried flower petals, or birdseed for guests to toss at the wedding couple. Put them in a basket for guests to pick up as they leave the ceremony, or have the flower girl and ring bearer hand them out to guests.

Favor bags can be made from paper, lace, or lightweight fabric. Boxes are made from wrapping paper, card stock, or origami paper. To speed construction, cut several layers of fabric or paper at a time, using a rotary cutter, ruler, and cutting mat. Line up seams of fabric or lace bags and feed them through the sewing machine one after the other, in a chain.

Making Paper Bag Favors

YOU WILL NEED

- DECORATIVE PAPER
- ROTARY CUTTER, MAT, AND STRAIGHTEDGE
- SCISSORS WITH DECORATIVE-EDGE BLADES
- SMALL BOX, SUCH AS FOR GELATIN, FOR FOLDING FORM
- CRAFT GLUE
- PAPER PUNCH
- NARROW RIBBON, FOR LACING
- NARROW RIBBON OR CORD, FOR HANDLE
- TISSUE PAPER

1 Cut 4" × 10" (10 × 25.5 cm) rectangle of paper for each bag. Trim one long edge, using scissors with decorative-edge blades, if desired.

2 Wrap paper around small box, lapping short edges; glue. Fold bottom edge, as for a gift, leaving decorative end open; glue. Remove box.

3 Punch even number of holes around upper edge; lace ribbon in and out of holes, and tie bow. Or, cut two pieces of ribbon, 6" (15 cm) long. Glue ends of ribbon to inside of bag, for handles. Embellish bag as desired.

4 Cut tissue paper, about 9" (23 cm) square. Pinch at center, and insert into bag. Fill bags, between folds of tissue paper.

Variations

ON THE THEME

LACE EDGING

Glue lace edging to upper edge of paper, before constructing bag.

EMBOSSED VELLUM

Emboss design onto front center, using embossing plate and stylus, before constructing bag. Curl ribbon ends and attach to outer surface of bag.

DECKLE EDGE

Tear paper, using deckle-edge ruler (page 22). Tear separate strip for upper edge; punch decorative holes in strip, if desired. Glue strip to upper edge; construct bag.

Making Fabric Bag Favors

YOU WILL NEED

- LIGHTWEIGHT FABRIC, SUCH AS LACE, SATIN, OR CREPE BACK SATIN
- RIBBON, 1/8" (3 MM) OR 1/4" (6 MM) WIDE
- EMBELLISHMENTS AS DESIRED
- HOT GLUE GUN

1 Cut fabric into 5" (12.5 cm) strips the entire width or length of fabric; cut ribbon into 9" (23 cm) strips.

2 Fold each fabric strip lengthwise, right sides together, matching raw edges. Stitch, using 1/4" (6 mm) seam allowance.

3 Lay tubes flat, centering seam. Stitch across one end of each tube 1/4" (6 mm) from end. Stitch across tube at 4" (10 cm) intervals.

4 Cut bags apart 1/4" (6 mm) below each stitching line, using pinking shears. Turn bag right side out.

Fill bags, and tie with ribbons, forming bows. Hot-glue desired embellishment over center of each bow. *5*

Making Lace Bag Favors

YOU WILL NEED

- GALLOON LACE (TWO SCALLOPED EDGES), 5" (12.5 CM) WIDE
- LIQUID FRAY PREVENTER
- PICOT-EDGED RIBBON, 1/4" (6 MM) WIDE

Cut galloon lace into 6 1/2" (16.3 cm) strips. *1*

Fold lace strip, right sides together, aligning cut edges. Stitch, using 1/4" (6 mm) seam allowance. At end of seam, do not remove lace from machine. Fold next lace strip and place under presser foot; stitch seam. Continue with remaining lace strips, forming chain. *2*

Apply liquid fray preventer to beginning and end of each seam; allow to dry. *3*

4 | Turn tubes right side out. Lay flat, centering seams, and stitch across one end of each tube, just above scallops.

5 | Fill bags, and tie with ribbons, forming bows.

Making Tulle Bag Favors

YOU WILL NEED

- TULLE OR ILLUSION FABRIC OR PRECUT TULLE CIRCLES, 6" (15 CM) DIAMETER
- 4 MM PEARLS
- FOIL-WRAPPED CHOCOLATE KISSES
- RIBBON, 1/8" (3 MM) OR 1/4" (6 MM) WIDE
- HOT GLUE GUN

1 | Cut 6" (15 cm) squares, if using netting; a rotary cutter is helpful. Or, use precut circles. Cut ribbon into 12" (30.5 cm) lengths.

2 | Place two kisses in center of each square or circle. Pull up ends of netting around kisses, and tie with ribbon.

3 | Hot-glue a pearl to bottom of each kiss, through netting, for bell clappers. Trim ribbon tails as desired.

YOU WILL NEED

- HEAVYWEIGHT WRAPPING PAPER, ORIGAMI PAPER, OR CARD STOCK
- ROTARY CUTTER AND STRAIGHTEDGE
- NARROW RIBBON; SEALING WAX

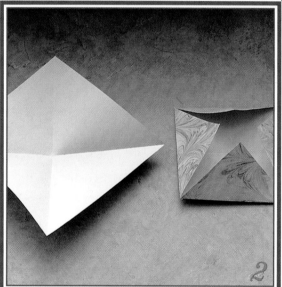

1

Cut paper squares, using rotary cutter. For 2" (5 cm) box lids, cut 5¾" (14.5 cm) squares; for 3" (7.5 cm) box lids, cut 8¼" (21.2 cm) squares. Cut box bottom squares ¼" (6 mm) smaller.

2

Fold square on diagonal; crease edge, and unfold. Fold and crease on other diagonal; unfold. Fold each corner of square to center; crease outer folds.

3

Fold one creased edge to center line; crease, and unfold. Repeat for remaining three sides, so that square, as folded in step 2, is divided into 16 squares.

Cut along inside horizontal edge of each corner square, stopping at inner fold line. Pull out two center flaps between cuts. | 4

Fold top and bottom rows to stand straight up; fold end squares in, butting edges. | 5

6 | Fold center flaps over sides to inside of lid.

7 | Repeat steps 2 to 6 to make box bottom. Fill box as desired; close box. Wrap length of narrow ribbon around box, crossing ends. Seal ribbon ends with sealing wax.

Historic Fact

IT WAS ONCE BELIEVED THAT EVIL SPIRITS WERE DRAWN TO WEDDINGS. SO, TO DISTRACT THEM, RICE WAS THROWN AT THE MARRIED COUPLE. TODAY, MANY VIEW BIRDSEED OR FLOWER PETALS AS A MORE ENVIRONMENTALLY CONSCIOUS CHOICE.

TABLE
Skirts

Softly gathered table skirts add a little coziness to a stark reception hall.

For a dramatic effect that can be achieved inexpensively, sew a swagged table skirt for the cake or buffet table. Select a woven fabric for the underskirt, and tulle for the swag. Create an elegant look by choosing all white fabrics, or customize the look by choosing a stripe, flower pattern, or solid color for the underskirt.

Historic Fact

IN ROMAN TIMES, THE WEDDING CAKE WAS BROKEN OVER THE BRIDE'S HEAD TO SYMBOLIZE A LIFE OF FRUITFULNESS, AND GUESTS SCRAMBLED TO PICK UP THE CRUMBS IN THE HOPES OF GAINING GOOD FORTUNE FOR THEMSELVES.

YOU WILL NEED

- WOVEN FABRIC, SUCH AS SATIN, TAFFETA, OR COTTON
- TULLE
- LARGE SAFETY PINS; RUBBER BANDS
- WIRED RIBBON, 2" (5 CM) WIDE, FOR BOWS, IF DESIRED
- FLOWERS, ARTIFICIAL OR FRESH, IF DESIRED

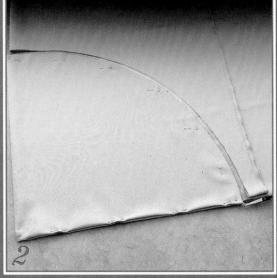

1 Cut one circle of fabric with diameter equal to tabletop plus 1" (2.5 cm). Cut one rectangle each of tulle and fabric with height equal to table height plus 1½" (3.8 cm) and width equal to two times table perimeter.

2 Fold circle into fourths; mark outer edge with short snips at folds. Open up circle.

3 Pin short ends of fabric rectangle, right sides together; stitch ½" (1.3 cm) seam, forming tube. Press seam open. Turn under and stitch double-fold ⅜" (1 cm) hem at lower edge. Repeat for tulle rectangle, but omit hemming. Pin wrong side of tulle tube over right side of fabric tube along top edge. Fold into fourths; mark edge with short snips at folds. Sew two rows of gathering stitches scant ½" (1.3 cm) and ¼" (6 mm) from top edge; for easier gathering, start and stop stitching at each quarter mark.

4 Pin circle to upper edge of skirt, right sides together, matching marks. Pull up gathering threads, distributing gathers evenly; pin. Stitch ½" (1.3 cm) seam; trim.

5 Place skirt over table; mark three or four evenly spaced points around upper edge for swags, placing one mark at seam.

6 Form swags, opposite. Secure ribbon bow or artificial or fresh flowers over pins or rubber bands.

BUNTING SWAGS
Fanfold tulle at each mark, from bottom edge to 5" (12.5 cm) from top of table; pin in place, using large safety pin. Adjust swags as desired.

TEARDROP SWAGS
Place hands on either side of point marked at bottom edge of tulle, and fold tulle up toward top, allowing teardrop to form between hands; secure with rubber band. Adjust height of swags as desired.

Sewing a Skirt for a Square or Rectangular Table

1 Follow steps 1 to 4 opposite, except use a rectangular piece for tabletop. Round corners to fit table, if necessary.

2 Place skirt over table; mark two or more points evenly spaced along front and back of table for swags. Plan a swag at each end. Complete as in step 6, opposite.

CHERISHED
MEMORABILIA

Treasured memories, like favorite photographs and faded flowers, hold a special place in your heart. With careful preservation and creative presentation, their freshness endures.

FABRIC-COVERED
Picture Frames

A fabric-covered picture frame is a lovely way to display a favorite wedding photo.

Create a custom picture frame using luxurious fabrics, trims, and some heavyweight cardboard. Cut your own frame to a custom size, or use a precut mat board.

Choose a firmly woven lightweight to mediumweight fabric, such as satin, moiré taffeta, or shantung. For construction ease, back the fabric with lightweight fusible interfacing. Lightly pad the frame with polyfleece, if desired, or select a flannel-backed satin as the covering fabric.

Embellish covered frames to complement the photograph, using ribbons, decorative cording, and beaded trims, if desired. Other embellishment ideas include ribbon roses, ribbon embroidery, and pearls.

YOU WILL NEED

- FABRIC
- POLYFLEECE, OPTIONAL
- LIGHTWEIGHT FUSIBLE INTERFACING
- HEAVYWEIGHT CARDBOARD, SUCH AS MAT BOARD OR ILLUSTRATION BOARD
- PRECUT MAT FOR FRAME FRONT, OPTIONAL

- DOUBLE-STICK TAPE
- FABRIC GLUE; FLAT PAINTBRUSH OR SPONGE APPLICATOR
- AEROSOL FABRIC ADHESIVE
- HOT GLUE GUN
- EMBELLISHMENTS AS DESIRED
- CLEAR ACETATE SHEET

1 Determine desired size of frame and opening; opening should be slightly smaller than photograph. Mark dimensions on cardboard for frame front, or use precut mat.

2 Mark dimensions of frame back on cardboard ½" (1.3 cm) narrower and shorter than frame front. Cut frame, using a few medium-pressure cuts per side rather than one heavy cut. Cut clear acetate sheet, if desired, to size of photograph.

3 Mark outer edge and opening of frame front on wrong side of fabric, using pencil or chalk. Cut fusible interfacing to match marked area; fuse, following manufacturer's directions. Cut fabric 1" (2.5 cm) beyond outer marked line and inside marked opening. Trace frame back on wrong side of fabric; cut fabric 1" (2.5 cm) outside marked lines. Trace back again; cut ⅛" (3 mm) inside marked lines.

4 Apply polyfleece, if desired, to frame front, using aerosol fabric adhesive; trim polyfleece even with edges of cardboard.

5 Center frame front, right side down, on wrong side of fabric; clip fabric at corners of opening to within scant ⅛" (3 mm) of cardboard. Apply double-stick tape along edges of opening; reinforce corners as shown. Wrap fabric through opening to back of frame; secure to cardboard. Clip fabric as necessary to fit curved opening.

Apply double-stick tape along outer edges. Wrap fabric firmly around frame edge, pinching fabric together at corners as shown. Fold excess fabric at corners flat; secure with fabric glue.

6

Apply smaller piece of fabric to frame back, using aerosol adhesive. Center frame back, fabric side up, on wrong side of remaining fabric piece; secure with spray adhesive. Tape and wrap sides as for frame front. Seal raw edges of fabric with diluted fabric glue; this is inside of frame back.

7

8

Apply glue to inside of frame back along three edges; center frame back on frame front, and secure. One side of frame is left open for inserting photograph.

9

Make and attach frame stand, if desired, as on page 166, steps 1 to 5.

Embellish frame edges with ribbon trim, gathered lace, or beaded trim as desired. Embellish frame front as desired. Insert photograph and protective clear acetate sheet, through open side.

10

Tip

THE FRAME SHOULD ENHANCE THE PHOTO, NOT OVERPOWER IT. USE SUBTLE COLOR IN THE FABRIC THAT DRAWS YOUR EYE TO DETAILS IN THE PHOTO.

Making a Frame Stand

1   Mark dimensions of frame on paper; divide rectangle in half diagonally. Measuring from lower corner, mark point on each side of corner a distance equal to about one-third the width of frame. Align a straightedge with one point and opposite corner; mark line from point to diagonal marked line. Repeat for remaining point.

2   Cut out frame stand pattern; trace on cardboard, and cut out. Lightly score cardboard ½" (1.3 cm) from upper edge, using straightedge and mat knife. Flip stand over and gently crease.

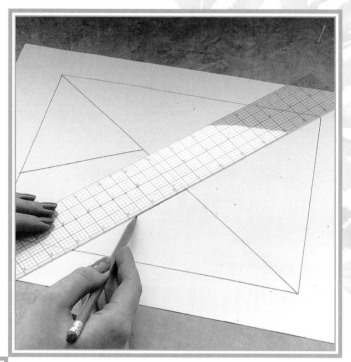

3   Position stand on wrong side of fabric, scored side up; trace. Cut ½" (1.3 cm) outside marked lines. Turn stand over, and trace on fabric. Cut ⅛" (3 mm) inside marked line, for lining piece.

4   Center stand, scored side up, on wrong side of larger fabric piece. Apply double-stick tape to edges; wrap fabric around edges, clipping at corners. Spray lining piece with aerosol adhesive; secure to wrong side of stand. Seal raw edges of fabric with diluted fabric glue.

5   Apply glue to lining side of frame stand above scored line. Secure stand to back of frame, aligning outer edges to frame corner.

Variations
ON THE THEME

PLEATED CORNERS
Accent the corners of a satin-covered frame with pleated fabric for an elegant, yet understated look.

NOSTALGIA
Secure a ribbon-tied arrangement of dried rosebuds and baby's breath in the lower corner of a frame covered with silk shantung.

SIMPLE CHIC
Cover the frame with crinkled organza. Wrap strings of tiny seed beads around each side of the frame for a little sparkle.

FABRIC-COVERED

Photo

Albums

GUEST BOOKS
& VIDEO CASES

Customize treasured keepsake books by covering them with fabric; do the same with the case that holds the videocassette of the wedding.

For a formal look, use satin, shantung, moiré taffeta, or brocade. If you prefer lightweight or slippery fabric, stabilize it with fusible interfacing. Apply thin batting or flannel under the fabric for a slightly padded appearance.

Create a dimensional effect with a padded silk ribbon embroidery design. Or, select a favorite photograph, and transfer it to fabric for the cover of a photo album. If you do not have a color printer at home, take the photograph to a professional copier. Be sure to bring written permission from the photographer, if you are using a professional wedding photo.

YOU WILL NEED

- BINDER-STYLE PHOTO ALBUM OR GUEST BOOK
- FABRIC
- THIN BATTING OR FLANNEL, OPTIONAL
- RIBBON FOR TIES, ½" (1.3 CM) WIDE, OPTIONAL
- THIN CARDBOARD
- CRAFT GLUE

1 Cut fabric strip with length equal to height of album plus 3" (7.5 cm). For album with centered rings, cut width is equal to width of spine plus 3" (7.5 cm). For album with rings attached to back cover, cut width is equal to width of spine plus width of ring base plus 3" (7.5 cm). On fabric back, mark size and location of ring base, keeping 1½" (3.8 cm) margin. Cut through center of marked rectangle, stopping ½" (1.3 cm) from ends; clip diagonally to corners.

2 Press under fabric along marked lines. Apply diluted glue sparingly to album, over area to be covered. Secure fabric strip over ring base; smooth out over spine and onto inside covers. Wrap and secure fabric to outside at top and bottom.

3 Cut batting, if desired, to measurements of open album. Apply diluted glue to outer covers and spine, avoiding 2" (5 cm) at ends of spine and behind ring base; secure batting.

4 Cut fabric 4" (10 cm) larger than open album. Center open album on wrong side of fabric. For album with centered rings, clip fabric to album edge at top and bottom folds of spine. For album with rings attached to back cover, clip to front fold of spine and to right side of ring base.

5 Fold fabric in between clips so raw edges meet album edges. Fold over again, tucking folded edge to outside and encasing batting, if used. Glue fabric to outer album surface.

Fold fabric to inside at corners; glue in place. Close album to make sure fabric is not too tight. Fold fabric on three edges of each cover to inside, mitering corners and folding fabric diagonally away from clips; glue in place.

6

Cut two 18" (46 cm) lengths of ½" (1.3 cm) ribbon, if ties are desired. Glue ribbon from center to edge on inside of each cover, leaving ties.

7

8 Cut two pieces of lightweight cardboard ⅜" (1 cm) smaller than inside covers. For album with rings attached to back cover, measure for back piece from right side of ring base. Cut two fabric pieces 4" (10 cm) larger than cardboard.

9 Apply diluted glue to front cardboard; center fabric over cardboard, and smooth to edges. Fold fabric to back at corners; glue in place. Fold fabric on edges to back, mitering corners; glue in place. Repeat for back cardboard.

10 Center cardboard pieces over inside covers; glue in place. Close album, and allow to dry thoroughly.

Making a Padded Silk Ribbon Embroidery Design

YOU WILL NEED

- MATERIALS FOR COVERING ALBUM (PAGE 170)
- FABRIC FOR EMBROIDERED DESIGN
- EMBROIDERY FLOSS IN DESIRED COLOR
- SILK RIBBON, 4 MM WIDE, IN DESIRED COLORS
- CHENILLE NEEDLE, SIZE 20 OR 22
- EMBROIDERY NEEDLE
- HEAVY CARDBOARD
- CRAFT GLUE
- DECORATIVE CORDING
- LACE EDGING, OPTIONAL

1 Cover album as on pages 170 and 171. Cut desired size ovals from cardboard and batting. Trace embroidery pattern onto right side of fabric; trace oval onto wrong side.

2 Embroider stems and letters in stem stitch (page 74), using an embroidery needle and two stands of embroidery floss. Embroider spiderweb roses (page 75), using chenille needle and silk ribbon; embroider leaves in Japanese ribbon stitch (page 73).

1

3 Cut out embroidered design ½" (1.3 cm) beyond marked line. Glue batting to cardboard; place batting side down over back of design. Clip outer edge of design every ½" (1.3 cm) up to cardboard. Apply diluted craft glue to cardboard edge; wrap clipped fabric edge over cardboard edge to secure.

4 Glue padded design to album front cover. Glue decorative cording and lace around outer edge of oval.

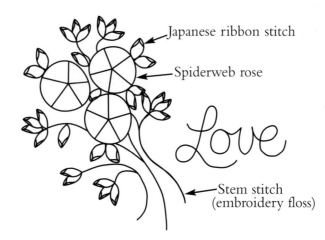

Japanese ribbon stitch

Spiderweb rose

Love

Stem stitch
(embroidery floss)

YOU WILL NEED

- MATERIALS FOR COVERING ALBUM (PAGE 170)
- WEDDING PHOTOGRAPH
- PHOTO TRANSFER PAPER
- ACCESS TO A COLOR PHOTOCOPIER
- LIGHTWEIGHT, TIGHTLY WOVEN 50% TO 100% COTTON FABRIC FOR THE TRANSFER
- IRON
- LACE FRAME
- FABRIC GLUE
- NARROW RIBBON

1 | Cover album as on pages 170 and 171. Photocopy photo onto photo transfer paper, using color copier.

2 | Iron transfer onto tightly woven cotton fabric, following manufacturer's instructions.

3 | Cut transferred photo slightly larger than opening in lace frame. Secure photo under frame opening, using fabric glue.

4 | Secure lace-framed photo onto album front, using fabric glue. Glue narrow ribbon around outer edge of lace frame, if desired.

Covering a Videocassette Box

YOU WILL NEED

- CLEAR PLASTIC VIDEOCASSETTE CASE
- ¼ YD. (0.25 M) FABRIC
- ¼ YD. (0.25 M) LINING FABRIC
- ¼ YD. (0.25 M) THIN BATTING OR FLANNEL
- ¼ YD. (0.25 M) RIBBON, 1½" (3.8 CM) WIDE
- ¼ YD. (0.25 M) RIBBON, 1" (2.5 CM) WIDE
- ⅔ YD. (0.63 M) RIBBON FOR TIES, ¼" (6 MM) WIDE, OPTIONAL
- 1⅓ YD. (1.27 M) GATHERED LACE OR RIBBON, OPTIONAL
- CARDBOARD, CEREAL-BOX WEIGHT, ABOUT 8" × 11" (20.5 × 28 CM)
- FABRIC GLUE

1 Glue 1½" (3.8 cm) wide ribbon to outside spine of cover, turning ends under. Fold long edges of ribbon over to front and back of case; glue to case. Glue 1" (2.5 cm) ribbon to remaining three sides, turning ends under. Cut lining fabric to fit inside box; glue in place.

2 Cut two 12" (30.5 cm) lengths of ¼" (6 mm) ribbon, if ties are desired. Glue each ribbon from center of case to outside edge on front and back cover, leaving 9" (23 cm) ties.

3 Cut two pieces of cardboard and batting same size as case front. Cut two pieces of fabric 2" (5 cm) longer and wider.

Glue batting to cardboard. Lay cardboard, batting side down, on wrong side of fabric so fabric extends 1" (2.5 cm) beyond cardboard on all sides. Fold corners of fabric, then fabric edges, to back side of cardboard; glue in place. Repeat for other cardboard. *4*

Glue gathered edge of ribbon or lace to back side edge of each cardboard, if desired. Glue cardboard pieces to case front and back. Embellish front cover as desired. *5*

Variations
ON THE THEME

EMBROIDERED DOILY

Embroider a large spiderweb rose (page 75) in the center of a heart-shaped doily. Accent with leaves, using the lazy daisy stitch (page 73). Secure the doily to a fabric-covered album, using fabric glue or hand stitches.

EMBROIDERY KITS

Kits for fabric-covered books, like this original design by Karen Timm, can be purchased by mail (see sources, page 192).

PHOTO TRANSFER

Transfer a favorite wedding photo to fabric, and secure it to a fabric-covered video case, using fabric glue. Conceal the raw edge with decorative cording.

MONOGRAM

Fuse your monogram appliqué, and hand-stitch a scattering of tiny pearls to fabric before covering the album.

DRIED WEDDING
Wreath

Flowers from the wedding can be dried and put into
a wreath as a lasting reminder of the special day.

Create a sentimental wreath using preserved flowers from the bridal bouquet, cake top, centerpieces, altar bouquets, and pew or arbor decorations. The wreath can be hung on the door or a wall or used to adorn a shelf or tabletop.

Preserve flowers in silica gel to retain the appearance of fresh flowers; they will keep their original size and shape, although colors may change slightly. Or air dry flowers for a romantic look; colors will soften, petals will take on a textured appearance, and flowers will shrink slightly. Alternatively, have flowers commercially freeze-dried to retain their shape and color; for a service company, check the florist section of the telephone directory under preserved flowers. Whichever method you choose, preserve flowers as soon as possible after the wedding for best results. Store flowers in a sealed bag in the refrigerator, if a delay is unavoidable.

Embellish the wreath with additional flowers dried from the garden or purchased from floral shops and craft stores, and use leftover ribbon or lace from the wedding dress or decorations.

For a base, choose a wire form or a grapevine wreath. Prolong the wreath's beauty by hanging or placing it away from humidity and direct sunlight.

Covering a Wire Form Wreath

YOU WILL NEED

- WIRE WREATH BASE
- FRESH SALAL OR BOXWOOD
- DRIED FLOWERS FROM THE WEDDING, PLUS ANY OTHERS DESIRED
- TRIMS, SUCH AS LACE OR RIBBON FROM WEDDING DRESS OR DECORATIONS
- RIBBON
- HOT GLUE GUN
- 22-GAUGE OR 24-GAUGE PADDLE FLORAL WIRE, CUT IN LENGTHS OF 15" TO 18" (38 TO 46 CM)
- SCISSORS AND WIRE CUTTER

1 Take flower bouquets or arrangements apart and dry as on pages 182 and 183, or commercially freeze-dry flowers. Dry additional flowers or purchase extra dried flowers, if desired. Cut fresh salal into lengths ranging from 6" to 8" (15 to 20.5 cm).

2 Trace inside and outside perimeter of wreath onto paper. Arrange greens and flowers on paper tracing, distributing flowers individually or in clusters around wreath. When a pleasing design is achieved, remove greens, but leave flowers on paper to use as a pattern.

3 Loop and tie a length of wire onto back of wire form, for hanging. Cluster four to six lengths of salal together, and wrap with wire. Place cluster on wire base; secure by wrapping wire from cluster around the base, crossing it in back, and twisting ends together in front. Secure additional salal clusters to base, overlapping each to conceal wire, until entire base is covered.

4 Move flowers from paper tracing to wreath, and hot-glue in place. Hot-glue clusters together before securing to wreath, and tie with ribbon or lace, if desired. Weave ribbon throughout wreath; secure with hot glue.

5 Hang wreath in desired location, and allow to dry. Rotate wreath occasionally while drying, so leaves curl evenly around the wreath's natural curve.

Covering a Grapevine Wreath

YOU WILL NEED

- GRAPEVINE WREATH
- SHEET MOSS
- DRIED FLOWERS FROM THE WEDDING, PLUS ANY OTHERS DESIRED
- TRIMS, SUCH AS LACE OR RIBBON FROM WEDDING DRESS OR DECORATIONS
- RIBBON
- HOT GLUE GUN
- 22-GAUGE PADDLE FLORAL WIRE FOR HANGER
- SCISSORS AND WIRE CUTTER

1 Dry flowers and design wreath as in steps 1 and 2, opposite. Loop and tie a length of wire onto back of wreath, for hanging.

2 Secure sheet moss to top and sides of grapevine wreath, using hot glue. Mist sheet moss lightly before securing to make it more pliable.

3 Hot-glue flowers and desired embellishments to wreath as in step 4, above.

AIR DRYING FLOWERS

HANG UPSIDE DOWN

Most varieties, including roses, can be hung upside down. Bundle stems together loosely, staggering heads so air can circulate evenly. Secure ends of stems together with rubber band and hang to dry in dark, dry, well-ventilated room.

VASE

Dry baby's breath, Queen Anne's lace, mimosa, delphiniums, and hydrangea upright in a vase with 2" (5 cm) of water; remove lower leaves. Water evaporates, leaving flowers preserved.

WIRE MESH

Place roses or other flowers with a large head on wire mesh placed over a deep box. Insert flower stems through mesh, allowing flower heads to rest on mesh. Support flower heads with tissue paper, if necessary. Place in dark, dry, well-ventilated room.

YOU WILL NEED

- AIRTIGHT CONTAINER, DEEPER THAN HEIGHT OF FLOWER HEADS PLUS 2" (5 CM), WITH COVER
- SILICA GEL
- AEROSOL FLORAL SEALER
- SMALL BRUSH

1

Cut stems to within 1" (2.5 cm) of flower heads. Fill container with silica gel, to a depth of 2" (5 cm). Place flowers in silica gel, and gently sprinkle silica gel between flower petals; then cover flowers completely.

2

Cover tightly with lid; allow to dry for two to seven days. Check daily, while drying, so flowers do not overdry and become brittle; tip container and gently pour some of the silica gel onto newspaper. When flowers are visible, gently lift them from silica gel with slotted spoon.

3

When dry, remove flowers from container, as in step 2, and brush excess silica gel from flower petals, using a soft brush. Attach any fallen petals with glue. Spray flowers with aerosol floral sealer to strengthen them. Dry silica gel, following manufacturer's directions, so it can be reused.

Cherished Memorabilia

HEIRLOOM
Shadow Box

Showcase treasured mementos of the engagement, wedding, or honeymoon in a glass-encased display.

Shadow box frames have deep sides that allow you to mount dimensional items, such as bows from shower gifts, a garter, gloves, or a wedding favor, as well as flat items, such as the newspaper announcement of the engagement, the wedding invitation, a photograph, or a postcard from the honeymoon. For a romantic touch, preserve flowers from the wedding, as on pages 182 to 183, and add them to the shadow box.

To determine the size of the shadow box that is needed, arrange all the objects to be mounted on paper, making sure to allow the desired amount of space around each item. Outline the items on the paper to record the placement, and mark and measure the frame size. To determine the frame depth, measure the deepest item and add ½" (1.3 cm) to allow for frame assembly. Order the shadow box and glass to these measurements from a frame shop. Acid-free foam-core board, wrapped with a natural-fiber fabric, is used for the mounting board and to line the inside of the frame.

Photographs, cards, and newspaper announcements can be hinge-mounted using linen framer's tape; mount on foam-core board first, then add a purchased frame mat, if desired. Many other items can be attached with hand stitches using thread that matches the item or monofilament fishing line for extra strength. Mount other items with silicone glue or plastic clips, available at frame stores.

The Commonwealth
of **The Bahamas**

This day I will marry my friend
the one I laugh with, dream with, live for and love . . .

YOU WILL NEED

- WOODEN SHADOW BOX
- NATURAL-FIBER FABRIC, SUCH AS 100% SILK, COTTON, OR LINEN
- 1/4" (6 MM) ACID-FREE FOAM-CORE BOARD
- DOUBLE-STICK FRAMER'S TAPE, OR ADHESIVE TRANSFER GUM (ATG) TAPE
- GUMMED LINEN FRAMER'S TAPE

- CLEAR ACRYLIC FINISH; PAINTBRUSH
- UTILITY KNIFE; CORK-BACKED METAL STRAIGHTEDGE
- NEEDLE, THREAD, FISHING LINE, THIMBLE, CLEAR SILICONE GLUE, MOUNTING CLIPS, SUCH AS MIGHTY MOUNTS™, AS NEEDED FOR MOUNTING VARIOUS ITEMS

- BACKING PAPER
- FRAMER'S FITTING TOOL OR SLIP-JOINT PLIERS
- AWL
- 3/4" (2 CM) BRADS
- SCREW EYES
- HANGING WIRE
- RUBBER BUMPERS

1 Seal any unfinished wood, using clear acrylic finish; allow to dry. Place glass in shadow box.

2 Mark strip of foam-core board 1/8" (3 mm) shorter and 3/8" (1 cm) shallower than inside top dimensions of shadow box. Score foam-core board repeatedly on marked lines, using utility knife and straightedge, until cut through. Repeat to cut inside bottom strip.

3 Cut fabric 2" (5 cm) larger than dimensions of each strip of foam-core board. Secure double-stick framer's tape to foam-core board along all outer edges. Center foam-core board, tape side up, on wrong side of fabric. Wrap fabric firmly around long sides; press in place onto tape.

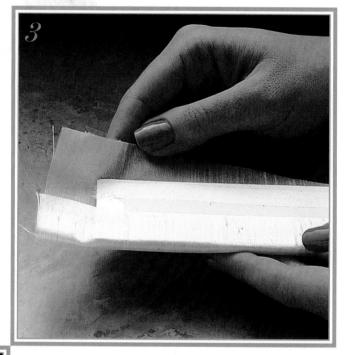

4 Wrap fabric around ends, folding mitered corners; secure to tape. Secure folded fabric at corners, using moistened strips of linen framer's tape.

5 Position top and bottom pieces in frame; pieces should fit snugly without buckling. Repeat steps 2 to 4 for the side pieces. Check fit of all pieces; if necessary, adjust size by peeling back fabric, then trimming foam-core board and rewrapping it.

6 Cut mounting board 1/4" (6 mm) smaller than frame opening dimensions. Wrap mounting board with fabric as in steps 3 and 4. Check fit of mounting board; adjust, if necessary.

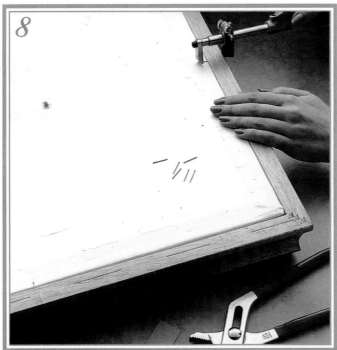

7 Remove glass and clean it on both sides thoroughly, using glass cleaner and lint-free cloth. Reposition glass in frame. Cut strips of double-stick framer's tape; secure to back of each piece for sides of frame. Secure top and bottom pieces to frame, then side pieces.

8 Attach items to mounting board, as on pages 188 and 189. Place mounting board in frame. Insert ¾" (2 cm) brads into middle of each side of frame, using framer's fitting tool as shown. Or use slip-joint pliers, protecting outside edge of frame with strip of cardboard. Recheck display and glass for lint, and remove brads if necessary to clean glass.

9 Insert brads along each side, 1" (2.5 cm) from corners and at about 2" (2.5 cm) intervals.

10 Cut backing paper 2" (5 cm) larger than frame dimensions. Attach double-stick transfer tape to back of frame, about ⅛" (3 mm) from outside edges; remove paper covering.

11 Place paper on back of frame, securing it to center of each edge of frame and stretching paper taut. Working from center out to each corner, stretch paper and secure to frame. Crease paper over outside edge of frame. Using a straightedge and utility knife, trim paper about ⅛" (3 mm) inside creased line.

12 Mark placement for screw eyes, using an awl, about one-third down from upper edge; secure screw eyes into frame. Thread end of wire two or three times through one screw eye; then twist end onto itself. Repeat at opposite side, allowing slack in hanging wire; top of wire is usually about 2" to 3" (5 to 7.5 cm) from top of frame when hung.

13 Cover ends of wire with masking tape. Secure rubber bumpers to back of frame, at lower corners.

1 Mark dimensions of photograph or flat paper item on a stiff mounting board. Score mounting board repeatedly on marked lines, using utility knife and straightedge, until board is cut through.

2 Place item facedown on smooth, clean surface. Fold 1¼" (3.2 cm) strip of linen framer's tape, gummed side out, folding back ¼" to ½" (6 mm to 1.3 cm), depending on the size and weight of the photograph or paper item. Moisten short side of strip and secure to item near one end, with the folded edge of the strip a scant ⅛" (3 mm) below upper edge of item. Repeat at opposite end.

3 Moisten the remainder of the strip; secure item to mounting board, aligning outer edges.

PLASTIC CLIPS

Mark location for holder. Punch hole from back side of mounting board, using awl. Insert holder, and press seed nut into place. Trim post a scant ⅛" (3 mm) from nut, using utility scissors or pruning shears.

HAND STITCHES

Using thimble and needle threaded with matching thread or monofilament fishing line, secure item in several places through mounting board with hand stitches. On back of board, tie thread tails and secure to board with linen framer's tape.

CLEAR SILICONE GLUE

Secure lightweight items to mounting board with bead of clear silicone glue. Allow to dry for 24 hours before placing board into frame.

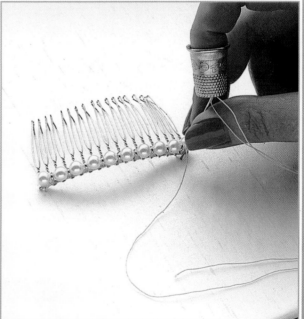

Tip

ADD HISTORICAL SIGNIFICANCE TO A SHADOW BOX BY INCLUDING WEDDING PHOTOS OF PARENTS AND GRANDPARENTS OR CHILDHOOD PICTURES OF THE BRIDE AND GROOM.

Cherished Memorabilia

Index

A

Accessories,
  see Bridal party accessories; Hair
    accessories
Aerosol adhesive, attaching stationery
  overlays, 15
Air drying flowers, 182-183
Albums, photo, fabric-covered, 168-174
Antique lace and beads on a headpiece, 48
Arbor, wedding, 120-123
Arch, lattice, flower-adorned, 123
Artificial flowers,
  cake tops, 142-144
  champagne bottle cover, 141
  corsages and boutonnieres, 108
  flower girl posy balls, 89-90
  hair wreaths, 50, 53
  mirror tile centerpieces, 130-133
  pew wreaths, 129
  table wreaths, 129
Attendant bouquets, 102-107

B

Bag, drawstring, 80-85
Bag favors, 148-153
Bakers, finding, 142
Barrettes and combs, 55-58
Baskets, 93-95
Beaded lace on a headpiece, 48
Bias binding edge finishes, 36-39
Birdcage card box, 137
Blusher veils, 28, 35
Bottle cover, champagne, 138-141
Bouffant veils, 28, 34
Bouquets, bridal and attendant, 102-107
Boutonnieres, 108-112
Bows,
  pew, tulle, 117
  shoe, 76

Box favors, 148, 154-155
Bridal bouquets, 102-107
Bridal garters, 63-67
Bridal party accessories,
  drawstring bag, 80-85
  edge finishes, 36-41
  garters, 63-67
  gloves, 78-79
  hair, 50-61
  headpieces, 42-49
  shoes, 68-77
  veils, 28-35
Bridal veils, 28
  blusher, 28, 35
  bouffant, 28, 34
  cascade, 28, 31-33
  edge finishes, 36-41
  headpieces, 42, 48
  lengths, 30
  underpouf support, 30
Buckram headpiece, 42, 44
Buckram pillbox hat, 42, 45
Bunting swags for table skirts, 159
Bun wrap headpiece, 42, 46

C

Cake tops, 142-145
Candle in a cloud centerpiece, 131
Cap, 59
Card holders, 134-137
Cascade veils, 28, 31-33
Centerpieces,
  floral table wreaths, 126-129
  mirror tile, 130-133
Ceremony accents,
  baskets, 93-95
  bridal and attendant bouquets, 102-107
  corsages and boutonnieres, 108-113
  flower girl posy balls, 88-92
  pew accents, 114-119

ring bearer pillows, 96-101
wedding arbor, 120-123
Chairs, slipcovered, 146-147
Champagne bottle cover, 138-141
Clips, shoe, 77
Combs and barrettes, 55-58
Corsages, 108-111, 113
Covers,
  chair slipcovers, 146-147
  champagne bottle, 138-141
Craft glue, attaching stationery
  overlays, 15

D

Deckled edges,
  on bag favors, 151
  on stationery, 22
Della Robbia effect on cake tops, 145
Die cutting stationery, 21
Drawstring bag, 80-85
Dried flower table wreath, 129
Dried wedding wreath, 178-183

E

Edge finishes, 36
  bias binding, 36-39
  pearl cotton, 41
  ribbon or lace, 41
  rippled, 40
  satin rattail, 41
Edges, deckled,
  on bag favors, 151
  on stationery, 22
Embossing stationery,
  pressure, 17
  thermal, 18
Embroidery kits for fabric-covered
  books and albums, 176

Embroidery, ribbon, 72-75
  on shoes, 71
Emergency kit, 41
Envelopes,
  see Stationery

F

Fabric bag favors, 152
Fabric-covered photo albums, guest
  books, and video cases, 168-177
Fabric-covered picture frames, 162-167
Fabric garters, 63-64, 67
Favors, table, 148-155
Finishes,
  see Edge finishes
Flower girl posy balls, 88-92
Flowers, pressed on stationery, 24
  also see Artificial flowers; Dried flower
  table wreath; Fresh flowers
Frames, picture, fabric-covered, 162-167
Fresh flowers,
  air drying, 182-183
  baskets, 95
  bouquets, 102-107
  cake tops, 142-144
  corsages and boutonnieres, 108-113
  dried and put into a wreath, 178-183
  flower girl posy balls, 89-90
  hair wreaths, 51-52
  mirror tile centerpieces, 130-133
  pew wreaths, 114
  table wreaths, 126-128
  wedding arbor, 120-123

G

Garters, 63-67
Gloves, 78-79
Glue stick, attaching stationery
  overlays, 14
Grapevine wreath, 181
Guest books, fabric-covered, 168-174

H

Hair accessories,
  barrettes and combs, 55-58

cap, 59
  headbands, 59-61
  wreaths, 50-54
Hair, styling, 35, 61
Hats, 42, 45, 59
Headbands, 59-61
Headpieces, 42
  buckram, 44
  bun wrap, 46
  pillbox hat, 45
  securing, 48
  various decorations on, 48
  wire-frame, 47
Heart pillow, ring bearer, 100-101
Heirloom shadow box, 184-189
Historic wedding facts, 54, 58, 68, 101,
  122, 139, 155, 156
Holiday theme table wreath, 129
Hurricane lamp centerpiece, 133

I

Invitations,
  see Stationery

K

Kits,
  embroidery for fabric-covered books
    and albums, 176
  emergency, 41

L

Lace bag favors, 152
Lace ball, flower girl, 89, 92
Lace edge finish, 41
Lace garters, 65-66
Lattice arch, flower-adorned, 123
Lengths, bridal veil, 30

M

Mailbox, decorative card box, 137
Marzipan fruit on cake tops, 145
Memorabilia,
  dried wedding wreath, 178-183

fabric-covered photo albums, guest
  books, and video cases, 168-177
fabric-covered picture frames, 162-167
heirloom shadow box, 184-187
Mirror tile centerpieces, 130-133
Monogram on fabric-covered books
  and albums, 177
Mounting corners of stationery
  overlays, 14

N

Nylon illusion for bridal veils, 28

O

Overlays, attaching on stationery, 14-15

P

Padded card box, 135-136
Painting with watercolors on
  stationery, 20
Paper bag favors, 150
Papers, selecting for stationery, 12
Patchwork pillow, ribbon and lace, ring
  bearer, 96-98
Pearl cotton edge finish, 41
Petals, sprinkling, 93
Pew accents, 114
  ribbon accents, 119
  ribbon roses, making, 118
  swags, 119
  tulle bows, 117
  wreaths, 116
Photo albums, fabric-covered, 168-174
Photo transfers on fabric-covered books
  and albums, 174, 177
Picture frames, fabric-covered, 162-167
Pillbox hat, 42, 45
Pillows, ring bearer, 96-101
Postage for stationery, 23
Posy balls, flower girl, 88-92
Potpourri pillow, ring bearer, 98-99
Pressed flowers on stationery, 24
Pressure embossing stationery, 17

R

Reception cards,
  see Stationery
Receptions,
  cake tops, 142-145
  card holders, 134-137
  centerpieces, mirror tile, 130-133
  chairs, slipcovered, 146-147
  champagne bottle cover, 138-141
  table favors, 148-155
  table skirts, 156-159
  table wreaths, fresh floral, 126-128
Rectangular table, skirt for, 159
Response cards,
  see Stationery
Ribbon and lace patchwork pillow, ring
  bearer, 96-98
Ribbon and sealing wax, attaching
  stationery overlays, 14
Ribbon edge finish, 41
Ribbon embroidery, 72-75
  on shoes, 71
Ribbons,
  attaching stationery overlays, 14-15
  bows on shoes, 76
  edge finish, 41
  garter, 67
  making roses out of, 118
  on pews, 119
  weaving on stationery, 23
Ring bearer pillows, 96-101
Rippled edge finish, 40
Roses, ribbon, making, 118
Round table, skirt for, 158

S

Satin and pearls on a headpiece, 48
Satin rattail edge finish, 41
Sealing wax and ribbon, attaching
  stationery overlays, 14
Securing headpieces, 48
Sepia tones on stationery, 25
Shadow box, heirloom, 184-189
Sheer wrap on stationery, 25
Shoes, 68-77
Silica gel, drying flowers in, 183
Silk flower table wreath, 129
Skirts, table, 156-159
Slipcovered chairs, 146-147
Sneakers, dancing, 77

Sprinkling petals, 93
Square table, skirt for, 159
Stamping designs on stationery, 18
Stamps for stationery, 23
Stationery, 9, 16
  attaching overlays, 14-15
  basics, 10-13
  deckled edges, 22
  die cutting, 21
  embossing, 17-18
  envelopes, 13
  invitations, 13, 136
  painting with watercolors, 20
  postage, 23
  pressed flowers, 24
  receptions cards, 13
  response cards, 13
  selecting papers for, 12
  sepia tones, 25
  sheer wrap, 25
  stamping designs, 18
  stenciling, 19
  thank-you cards, 13, 136
  weaving ribbon, 23
Stenciling stationery, 19
Stickers, attaching stationery overlays, 15
Swags,
  on pews, 119
  on table skirts, 156, 159

T

Table favors, 148-155
Table skirts, 156-159
Table wreaths, 126-129
Teardrop swags, for table skirts, 159
Thank you cards,
  see Stationery
Thermal embossing stationery, 18
Tossing the garter, 67
Tulle bag favors, 153
Tulle bows on pews, 117
Twig arbor, 123
Twig ball, flower girl, 89, 91

U

Underpouf support, bridal veil, 30

V

Veils,
  see Bridal veils
Video cases, fabric-covered, 168, 175
Votive candleholder centerpiece, 132

W

Watercolors, painting stationery, 20
Weaving ribbon on stationery, 23
Wedding arbor, 120-123
Wedding wreath, dried, 178-183
Wire form wreath, 180-181
Wire-frame headpiece, 42, 47
Woven ribbon, attaching stationery
  overlays, 15
Wreaths,
  hair, 50-54
  pew, 116
  table, 126-129
  wedding, dried, 178-183

Sources

Clotilde, Inc.
(800) 772-2891
www.clotilde.com
sewing notions

Florilegium Needleart & Antiques
823 E. Johnson Street
Madison, WI 53703
(608) 256-7310
www.florilegium.com
fabric-covered books, page 176

Hues, Inc.
(800) 268-9841
www.huesinc.com
Photo Effects photo transfer paper

Mokuba Ribbons/MKB Ribbon
(212) 302-5010
www.festivegiftwrap.com

Signature Marketing & Manufacturing
(800) 865-7238
fabric glue; craft glue